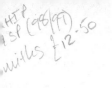

The Travel Industry in Britain

Pauline Horner

Stanley Thornes (Publishers) Ltd

First published in 1991 by:
Stanley Thornes (Publishers) Ltd
Ellenborough House
Wellington Street
CHELTENHAM GL50 1YW
United Kingdom

96 97 98 99 00 / 10 9 8 7 6 5

British Library Cataloguing in Publication Data

Horner, Pauline
The travel industry in Britain.
I. Title
338.4

ISBN 0–7487–0599–6

Typeset by Tech-Set, Gateshead, Tyne & Wear.
Printed and bound in Great Britain by Scotprint Ltd, Musselburgh

Contents

Introduction

This book is aimed at anyone who aspires to work in a travel agency. In particular, it is aimed at the trainee who is following the ABTA/City and Guilds 499 Certificate in Travel Studies course. The book will also be useful for students of the GCSE in Travel and Tourism; the Oxford Certificate of Travel and Tourism; the Travel and Tourism Environment and the Tour Operations units of the BTEC National Diploma in Travel and Tourism; and the Tourism units of the BTEC First and National Diplomas in Leisure Studies. It will also be of interest to anyone who would like to know more about the background of the travel and tourism industry.

The ABTA/City and Guilds 499 Certificate in Travel Studies course has several compulsory components:

◆ it is a one-year intensive course, with a minimum of 750 hours in College, studying travel related topics;

◆ students spend at least six weeks working in a travel agency;

◆ an educational visit to a foreign destination is normally included in the course.

The activities suggested in this book will presume that the reader has the above opportunities.

Students following the ABTA/City and Guilds 499 Certificate in Travel Studies course take four examinations:

1 Certificate in Travel Agency Competence 1 (COTAC 1) – Air
2 Certificate in Travel Agency Competence 1 (COTAC 1) – General
3 Travel Studies – General
4 Coursework Assessment

The first two COTAC examinations are concerned with the skills required in a travel agency. They deal, for example, with the travel agent's ability to advise clients on suitable travel arrangements by air; to complete an airline ticket; to book a car ferry crossing; to book a package holiday; to advise clients about necessary insurance, visas or health precautions.

This book is intended as an aid for the Travel Studies and Coursework Assessment examinations which deal with the background to the travel industry and the selling skills which are essential qualities in a travel agent. Topics covered in the book include:

◆ what is a travel agent?

◆ historical aspects of British tourism,

◆ organisations within the UK travel industry,

◆ travel geography and tourist destinations,

♦ tour operations and brochure production,

♦ cruising,

♦ marketing in travel,

♦ retail travel practices,

♦ selling skills in a travel agency.

The activities suggested within each chapter offer opportunities to extend your knowledge of the travel industry and to practise relevant skills. At the beginning of each chapter there is a short indication of the knowledge and skills included in the chapter.

The revision questions at the end of each chapter are in the style of the ABTA/City and Guilds 499 Certificate in Travel Studies examination. The answers to these questions are all contained in the text of the preceding chapter or are available through the experience gained in the suggested activities.

At the end of the book there is a glossary of terms and special words used in the travel industry. Within the text of the book, these words appear in **bold** type where appropriate.

Acknowledgements

The author and publisher wish to thank the following for permission to reproduce photographs and copyright material.

ABTA (p. 32); Access (p. 166); ANTOR (p. 29); Barclays Merchant Services (p. 166 Visa); BES Bradford (p. 23); BITOA (p. 30); Blackpool Tourism Dept. (p. 8); British Tourist Authority (p. 21); Civil Aviation Authority (p. 26); English Heritage (p. 24 and photo p. 25); English Tourist Board (p. 21); Gatwick Airport Ltd. (p. 27); ITT (p. 35); Leisure Sport Ltd/ Thorpe Park (p. 51); Mary Evans Picture Library (pp. 4, 15); National Trust (p. 29); Northern Ireland Tourist Board (p. 21); Ontario Tourism (p. 85); PATA (p. 30); PSA (p. 32); Royal Caribbean Cruises (pp. 138, 142); Scottish Tourist Board (p. 21); Sefton Council (pp. 5, 23); STB/Still Moving Picture Company (p. 45); Syndication International (p. 38); USTTA (pp. 78, 81); Wales Tourist Board (p. 21 and photos p. 44); Wigan Pier (p. 50).

All other photos were provided by the author.

Every effort has been made to contact copyright holders and we apologise if any have been overlooked.

1 *What is a Travel Agent?*

By the end of this chapter you should have increased your:

♦ **knowledge about the role of a travel agent;**

♦ **skills of observation**

An agent is a person who represents or works on behalf of another person or business. They are agents for their *client* who is booking a holiday or travel arrangement. They are also agents for the *company* on whose behalf they are making the booking, and from whom they will receive **commission** or payment.

> Commission is a payment to the agent usually made on a percentage basis. The travel agent can earn commission at varying rates depending on the company with which they are dealing. For example an airline would give 9 per cent commission, a tour operator would give 10 per cent and an insurance company could give 40 per cent or even more.

Here is an example:

> Mr and Mrs Armstrong come into Faraway Travel to book a holiday in Australia. They want return airline tickets from Manchester to Sydney with a stopover in Singapore. They need hotel accommodation in Singapore for two nights, and in Sydney for one night on both the outward and the return journeys. They will be staying with relatives in Australia during the rest of their holiday.

In this case, Faraway Travel are agents for the Armstrongs and make the booking on their behalf. The Armstrongs will receive from Faraway Travel the tickets and hotel confirmations together with a detailed itinerary of the times of their flights. Faraway Travel will also probably advise the Armstrongs that they will need full passports valid for 10 years, and if they are British, **visas** to visit Australia. Although the responsibility for actually applying for the visas rests with the Armstrongs themselves, the travel agency could arrange for them to receive the appropriate visa forms.

At the same time Faraway Travel are agents for the airline, and for the hotels with which they make the booking. They will receive commission or payment from these companies and will be expected to complete all the necessary paperwork to make the holiday possible.

Travel agents can make bookings with a variety of companies and these are referred to as **principals**. Some examples of principals are: airlines, British Rail, car ferry companies, cruise lines, **tour operators**, hotels, coach companies, theatres, etc.

Each principal will pay the travel agent to represent them and make bookings on their behalf. The amount paid by the principals varies, and in Chapter Twelve you will have the opportunity to look at the different commission levels available to the travel agent.

To summarise, the travel agent has two main roles:

1 *To give advice about:*
♦ destinations
♦ means of travel
♦ accommodation
♦ visas
♦ health precautions
♦ insurance

2 *To make bookings for:*
♦ independent travellers
♦ business travellers
♦ package holidaymakers
♦ theatre–goers

◇ Activity 1.1 ◇

1 Make a visit to a local travel agency and observe the following:
a) the window display,
b) the late availability cards in the window,
c) the display of brochures,
d) the number of staff,
e) the uniform of the staff,
f) the technology available to the staff,
g) the layout of the agency,
h) the attitude of the staff to their customers,
i) the attitude of the staff to each other.

2 Without inconveniencing the staff, try to discuss with them their role as travel agents. Ask them some of the following questions to encourage discussion:

♦ What training do the staff have?
♦ What hours do they work?
♦ Do they get cheaper holidays themselves?
♦ Do they like working in a job with the public?
♦ Do they like working with computers?
♦ What are the best aspects of the job?

3 If possible, make a visit to another travel agency and then compare the observations you made and discussions you have had.

2 *Historical Aspects of British Tourism*

By the end of this chapter you should have increased your:

 ♦ knowledge of the history of tourism over the past two centuries;
 ♦ skills with regard to UK locational geography;
 ♦ awareness of the influence of current political and social situations on tourism.

What is Tourism?

In its widest sense we could say that tourism is temporary or short term travel to a place, or places, other than where a person normally lives.

If people travel for only a day, we call them **excursionists**, but if they stay one or more nights, then we call them **tourists**. People become tourists or excursionists for many reasons:

 ♦ for relaxation, pleasure, health, or sport;

 ♦ for religious, cultural, educational or historical interests;

 ♦ for business;

 ♦ to visit friends and relatives and meet other people.

Indeed many people become tourists for more than just one of these reasons.

Wherever tourists spend their holidays there are usually certain facilities that they will expect to find. These are listed below.

 ♦ Help will be sought from a travel agent, or from the booking reservations staff of the airline, coach company or ferry operators to reach the destination.

 ♦ They will want somewhere to stay, such as a hotel, apartment or caravan.

 ♦ They will expect to find a restaurant or cafeteria in which to eat.

 ♦ Information will be sought about the place in which they are staying.

 ♦ Some form of entertainment will have to be provided.

All of these facilities imply jobs in the travel industry for those who are willing to meet the needs of the modern holidaymaker or business traveller.

The Early Growth of British Tourism

There are four essential components of tourism:

♦ travel,
♦ pleasure,
♦ leisure time,
♦ a travel industry.

Travel

In the earliest times people travelled to hunt and explore, or to make pilgrimages. However, travel alone does not make tourism. Since Roman times in Britain people have travelled to spa towns such as Bath, Harrogate and Scarborough to bathe in health-giving spring waters. In the early eighteenth century, however, people also began to visit the seaside to bathe in, and drink, sea water. Spa towns such as Scarborough, situated on the coast were in an ideal position to offer accommodation and other services to the new travellers. These towns already had an **infrastructure** of hotels, shops, cafes and in some cases a promenade because they were used to welcoming visitors.

By 1730 both Scarborough and Brighton were attracting visitors in quite large numbers, even though at this time Brighton was still two days' journey by coach and horses from London.

In 1815 steamboat services were introduced from London to the resorts of Gravesend and later Margate. We have a lasting memorial to the days of the steamboat in the piers which were built for them to land their passengers. The piers quickly became the focal point for the social life of the resorts and even to this day many piers still operate as centres for live entertainment. Entertainers still refer to doing a 'season' at a seaside resort and this recalls the time when it was fashionable to do a season at a spa in late August before attending the London Season at the end of the year.

A mini-train takes tourists to the end of the pier at Southport while the hovercraft lands passengers on the sand.

The word 'season' is still used in the travel industry when referring to booking periods in brochures, where for example the busiest holiday time in July and August is called the high season.

The steamboat as a means of travel had only a short life as it was overtaken by the railways a few years later. The popularity of the railways in the 1850s made travel in Britain easier and cheaper. This encouraged the growth of the seaside resorts which were the first centres of mass tourism in the UK.

The first passenger railway line in southern England was opened in 1830 between Canterbury and Whitstable. In the same year the Liverpool and Manchester Railway succeeded in covering the 31 miles between the two Lancashire cities in just an hour and a half.

When half-day closing was introduced in many towns in the 1890s, the railways were quick to seize the opportunity and offer excursions to the nearest seaside resorts.

Pleasure

In this country, travel for pleasure on a more or less organised scale, began with the Grand Tour in the eighteenth century. The Grand Tour was a visit abroad made by the sons and daughters of the rich when they reached their late teens. The visit could last up to three years and its purpose, apart from the pleasure of travelling and seeing the sights of Europe, was to educate and broaden the minds of the young people.

When the rich young people of the eighteenth century were doing their Grand Tour, ordinary working people in Britain had to make do with saints' feast days or holy days. This is the origin of the word 'holiday'. For ordinary people living in rural areas, a holy day meant a day, or even days, of rest with merrymaking and feasting. These occasions brought plenty of drink and meat, luxuries such as oranges and ribbons for the children, and time to be able to visit relatives in nearby villages. The feast days were sometimes celebrated at a local fair with entertainers and market stalls.

Leisure Time

With the coming of the Industrial Revolution in the late eighteenth century, some of the holy days of the rural life were lost, but employers in all areas of the country found it impossible to stop workers attending the larger festivals. These included traditional local festivals such as revels in the West Country, rushbearing in Lancashire and wakes weeks in Derbyshire and Staffordshire.

During these periods the mill or factory would shut down and all the workers had a holiday, even though it would have been an unpaid week. With the mill closed, local shops would also close and so the whole town might be 'on holiday' together. The time was used to visit relatives in the country and then, as seaside resorts developed, places like Blackpool depended on these holidays for their livelihood.

In 1871 Bank Holidays were first introduced, giving families guaranteed leisure time for at least a day at a time. Women and young people were granted six days paid holiday a year by the 1901 Factory Act. Some enlightened employers at the end of the last century actually gave all of their employees a paid holiday week each year. One such employer in Bristol said that he hoped it would contribute to the health and happiness of the workforce. However, this kind of generosity was not widespread, and it took the Holidays with Pay Act of 1938 to encourage voluntary agreements about paid holidays on a wide scale.

Statutory leisure time in the UK

1871	Bank Holidays were introduced
1890s	Half-day closing was introduced in some local areas
1901	Factory Act gave six days holiday a year to women and young people
1938	Holidays with Pay Act

The Travel Industry

A fourth ingredient of tourism is the travel industry itself which has developed in response to the needs of would-be tourists. Thomas Cook organised his first rail excursion from Leicester to Loughborough for 570 members of the Temperance Association in 1841. Ten years later he organised trips to the Great Exhibition in Hyde Park. One young visitor who travelled to the Great Exhibition with her parents in 1851 told of how

Thomas Cook had booked the hotel, the train, on which he even provided hot water-bottles, and, best of all, couriers and guides to help his clients at every step of the way.

The Paris International Exhibition in 1855 gave Thomas Cook the opportunity to offer continental trips and from there Cook's tours became ever more popular and adventurous. In 1872 at a price of 210 guineas Thomas Cook offered a round-the-world trip taking in Hong Kong, Singapore and India and lasting nearly a year. His son John Cook took the first American tour in 1886 and with his three grandsons carried on the successful business into this century.

Others naturally imitated the idea of packaged tours but some like the Cyclists Touring Club, founded in 1878, and the Toynbee Travellers Club put more emphasis on the educational value of the trips. In the 1880s, Sir Henry Lunn was responsible for organising lecture tours to Greece for his Nonconformist friends as well as some of the first skiing holidays to Switzerland.

It is interesting to read some of the letters to *The Times* at the turn of the century which show a prejudice on the part of the upper classes at seeing these groups of English people travelling around Europe together and attracting so much attention.

> Charles Lever, the British Vice-Consul at Spezia said that the cities of Italy were 'deluged with these creatures', whom he referred to as 'dowdy, uncouth, tossed, crumpled and facetious.'

Sadly, some of the letters also show the insular attitude of some tourists who expected to go abroad, yet find everything as English as possible. This has changed little even today, and most travel agents will tell you that they have met the type of client who goes to Italy for a holiday and then complains that the food was Italian!

By the end of the last century conditions existed for the development of mass tourism. These were as follows:

♦ ordinary people, not just the rich, had the leisure and time to indulge in tourism;

♦ transport networks, particularly railways, provided cheaper and easier means of travel;

♦ industrial workers earned money which they could spend on holidays of their choice;

♦ commercial organisations existed to arrange the opportunities for travel and tourism.

British Mass Tourism in this Century

The Seaside Resorts

We have already seen that seaside resorts were the first sites of mass tourism in the UK. In the north of England, the traditional wakes weeks were observed as holidays for entire towns until the 1950s.

The landladies of Blackpool could be sure of their clients throughout the season, as well as from year to year, in the first half of this century, because as one town's holiday week finished, so another would start.

Seaside resorts are still important today, although their role is changing. Many traditional seaside resorts are capitalising on their Victorian hotels and architecture and offering short breaks, family weekends and conference facilities in comfortable surroundings.

◇ Activity 2.1 ◇

1 So that you can begin to familiarise yourself with the position of some British seaside resorts, name the resorts and main towns marked with a dot on the map in Diagram 2.1 on the next page. The lines indicate the rail network – what does this tell you about the development of the seaside towns and of the railways?

2 Write for an information pack to some of the seaside resorts you have listed. In each case you could write to:

　　　　Tourist Information Centre
　　　　Resort 'X by the sea'
　　　　County 'Y'

When you receive the information packs, choose one resort, examine the information on it and look at the facilities on offer to tourists. Make a chart of information about the town showing for example:

♦ the number of four/three/two/one star hotels,

♦ hotels with swimming pools

♦ local sports facilities,

♦ details of any specialist restaurants,

♦ information about any unique attractions,

♦ is there a local folk museum?

♦ does the town offer short breaks?

♦ what are the conference facilities?

♦ do they offer theme breaks, such as 'Murder Weekends'?

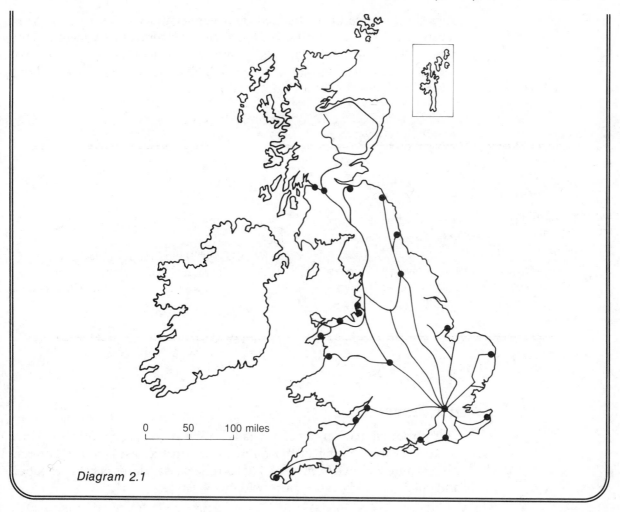

Diagram 2.1

0   50   100 miles

Holiday Camps

In the 1920s and 1930s private cars became more widespread and for those who could not afford a private car there were the coaches or charabancs.

This new means of transport encouraged cheaper holidays by the sea, for example in camps with tents or chalets. At this time the camps took up to 300 people but in 1935 Billy Butlin built his first holiday camp at Skegness in Lincolnshire to take 3000 guests.

Billy Butlin worked on the idea that he would make more money by taking a small profit from a lot of people, rather than a large profit from a few. This is an idea which still holds true in the travel industry today.

Once he had his first guests at Skegness, Billy Butlin could not understand why the faces around him were so glum when he had provided everything for their comfort and the beach was only a stone's throw away. It did not take him long to realise that these people were bored and so the famous red coats were born when he persuaded a friend to don a red blazer and organise some entertainment. Ever since, entertainment with resident red, blue or yellow coats has been a symbol of British holiday camps.

Holiday camps have changed their names and with it their image in recent years. They are now known as holiday centres or villages. Many centres have fun pools with slides and wave machines, and some have shed their family image and appeal to adults only. We will look at holiday centres in more detail in Chapter Four.

◊ *Activity 2.2* ◊

1 To help you get a picture of how holidays have changed over the years put the questions below to four people.

One person should be your own age, another your parents' age, the third the age of your grandparents and the fourth a person in their eighties.

These are the questions you should ask all four:

a) What is your earliest memory of a holiday?

b) As a child what did you do for a holiday?

c) What was your best holiday and why was it so good?

Air Travel

The introduction of air travel has had as great an impact on tourism in this century as the coming of the railways had in the last century. Foreign places came within easier reach and, as time passed, fares became cheaper and so air travel became more widely available.

> In 1929 it was realised that there was a need for international agreement on regulations for airline travel. In that year the Warsaw Convention agreed for the first time that airlines should be liable in the event of death or injury.

In 1944 eighty governments were represented at the Chicago Convention on Civil Aviation where standard operating procedures were discussed. It was here that the five freedoms of the air were recognised, with regard to:

1 the right to fly across another country without landing;

2 the right to land in a country, for example to refuel;

3 the right to off-load freight, mail or passengers from an aircraft of the country from which they originated;

4 the right to load freight, mail or passengers on to an aircraft of the country for which they are destined;

5 the right to load or off-load freight, mail and passengers on aircraft other than those of the country of destination or origin.

Since 1950 there have been several international agreements in relation to passenger safety, noise and pollution, and the fares to be charged on particular routes. The levels of compensation agreed at the Warsaw Convention in 1929 have also been amended as they were criticised by some states as being set too low. In fact the United States renounced the Warsaw Convention in 1965 in favour of higher levels of compensation. Consequently there are currently three agreements in operation – the Warsaw Convention, the Hague Protocol of 1955 and the Montreal agreements of 1975. However, the minimum levels of compensation established by the Warsaw Convention still apply, although higher levels may operate in some circumstances. Nowadays the largest international body is the International Air Transport Association (IATA) to which 80 per cent of the world's airlines belong.

Mass foreign holidays abroad have been made possible since the 1950s because of the availability of cheaper, faster travel by air. The Second World War had not only stimulated aircraft production and pilot training, but it had also given many people their first taste of 'being abroad'. In the immediate post-war years there was a surplus of aircraft which entrepeneurs such as Freddie Laker used to expand air travel to the masses. Fares were relatively high at first but the aircraft were comfortable, safe and much faster than those that had been available in the 1930s. 'Tourist' fares were introduced in 1952 and 'economy' fares in 1958. In the 1950s wider bodied jets were used for the first time on the scheduled, regular routes, so suddenly a lot of older aircraft were available on the market at cheap prices. These aircraft were bought and operated on a **charter** basis.

> Charter flights do not operate to a permanent timetable, as the scheduled airlines do, but are used to fly a full load of passengers to specific holiday destinations.

In operating their airlines in this way the new owners could be sure of filling their planes and could charge cheaper fares. Thus the cost of airline travel came within reach of the ordinary person. Once again, as in the early days of rail travel, resorts started to flourish – but this time it was the sunny resorts of Spain, such as Benidorm, that were to develop.

Package Holidays

Vladimir Raitz of Horizon is said to have been the first person to negotiate charter seats with an airline. The Horizon offices were opened in 1949 over a tobacconist's shop in Fleet Street. The first charter was of a thirty-two seater DC3 to Corsica. For £32.10 shillings each, the thirty-two clients were flown from London to Corsica and given full board accommodation in tents. Bearing in mind that the average wage per week in the 1950s was about £10, this holiday was not as cheap as it sounds, representing three weeks' wages. Nevertheless it was considerably cheaper and more convenient than travelling independently to Corsica.

A **package holiday** includes:

♦ the *transport* to the holiday destination,

♦ the *accommodation* throughout the holiday,

♦ the *transfer* from the airport or ferry, to the accommodation.

Package holidays are put together by **tour operators** who charge an all-in price for the whole holiday, and provide **couriers** to look after their clients during the holiday.

The idea of package holidays by air caught on fast during the 1950s and 1960s and by 1965 there were over a million holidays to western Europe from the UK using charter aircraft. Competition was fierce and prices were cut to a minimum with inevitable bankruptcies.

These included Fiesta Tours which was declared bankrupt in 1964. When clients flew into Perpignan, southern France for their holidays on the Costa Brava, Spain they found that their accommodation had not been paid for. Stranded holidaymakers were returned to Britain in spare seats on aircraft chartered by other ABTA members, but in some cases they had to draw lots for the seats.

ABTA or the Association of British Travel Agents was formed in 1950 in response to the need for travel agents and tour operators in this country to support each other in a new and growing industry. Chapter Three will give more detailed information about ABTA.

By 1967 a number of UK tour operators had gone out of business or had been taken over by larger companies. Of the remaining companies, the larger ones came together to form the Tour Operators Study Group (TOSG) to discuss travel issues of common interest. In 1994 TOSG

changed its name to the Federation of Tour Operators (FTO). FTO has nineteen members who between them are responsible for over 80 per cent of all overseas package holidays sold in the UK.

The Boeing 747 aeroplane, which can carry over 400 passengers, was developed in response to the greater number of people wishing to travel and came into regular service in 1970. That year there were over two million package holidays out of this country. By then there were ten large UK tour operators.

> The top four tour operators in 1970 were:
> - Clarksons,
> - Thomsons,
> - Horizon and
> - Cosmos.

The large operators continued to compete with each other, mainly by cutting prices to a minimum. Sometimes the companies offered holidays with no profit at all. In 1974 Clarksons offered an eight-day holiday to San Antonio in Ibiza for only £32 which was the price of Horizon's Corsica holiday 25 years before. However, with inflation, the average weekly wage had by then trebled to £30, making this holiday price ridiculously low.

The company which became a casualty this time was Court Line which by then owned both Clarksons and Horizon. The Court Line crash came at the height of the season in August, 1974 and it left many tourists, as well as employees, stranded abroad. The company's bond with ABTA was used to fly 35 000 people home but it seemed for a time that those who had booked holidays yet to be taken would not receive any compensation. Some employees of Court Line did not receive compensation until 1989!

To help those who had booked holidays with Clarksons, the government stepped in with a loan to create the Air Travel Reserve Fund which paid out compensation. The fund still exists today, although it is now called the Air Travel Trust, and it is administered by the TOSG which was mentioned above. This fund was used in 1991 to fly home clients of Intasun after its parent company, International Leisure Group (ILG) was unable to pay its landing bills at Gatwick Airport because of financial difficulties.

In spite of setbacks such as the Court Line crash, the package holiday trade continued to grow throughout the 1970s and 1980s. Figures from the Department of Employment in the International Passenger Survey give the number of visits by UK residents on holiday inclusive tours. These show:

- two million package holidays were offered in 1970,
- six million holidays were offered in 1980,
- nine million holidays were offered in 1984,
- ten million holidays were offered in 1986,
- and over 12 million holidays were offered in 1988.

The graph below shows how 1988 was, in fact, a peak year for package holidays. Since then, fear of terrorism, aircraft defects, flight delays and then the Gulf War in 1991 have all combined to discourage tourists from taking as many package holidays.

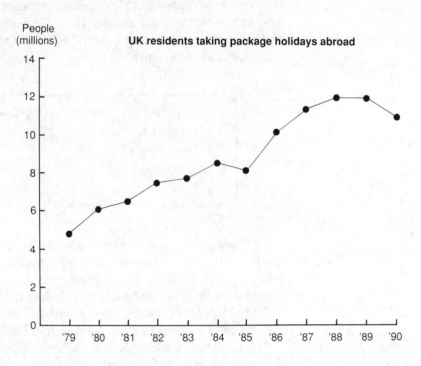

In the 1980s package holidays to the USA, Australia and the Far East became popular and more available. It is possible to find **self-catering holidays** in these more exotic destinations for the same price as one would pay for an average to good European hotel package.

The travel industry market is specialising or segmenting more and more with brochures offering skiing or golfing holidays, weekend breaks or **fly/drive**. Some of these brochures are offered by the big companies but many are products of the small specialist tour operators which make up the bulk of the ABTA tour operator membership. In Chapters Seven, Eight and Nine we will study tour operations, the costing of brochures and the position of the tour operator before the law if things go wrong with a holiday.

Cruising

In the last century, as the British Empire grew, regular shipping routes were opened up from about 1840 onwards. P & O operated about 60 ships to India and the Far East, and Cunard's ships took both first class and steerage passengers across the Atlantic. On the luxury liners at the turn of the century, the first class passengers travelled in style as if they were in a luxury hotel. However, the steerage passengers who were emigrating to the New World travelled in very basic conditions with only dormitories often below the water line.

Steerage passengers emigrating to the New World, 1872.

For over twenty years, from 1906, the Cunard ship
Mauritania held the coveted Blue Riband trophy for the
fastest trans-Atlantic sea crossing at 26 knots. In the
1930s the *Queen Mary* reached even faster speeds, with
a record 31 knots in 1936.

By the end of the 1930s Cunard could offer ten-weekly crossings of the
Atlantic. At this time the 'tourist' class of travel was introduced, mainly to
appeal to the American middle classes who were beginning to travel to
Europe and take package holidays touring on the Continent.

All of this changed however when the new jet aircraft made air travel
both faster and cheaper and travel by ocean liner declined.

- ◆ In 1958 1 200 000 passengers crossed the Atlantic by
  ship, but in the same year Boeing 707 aeroplanes
  came into regular service.
- ◆ In 1959 Cunard lost 25 per cent of its passengers to
  the airlines.
- ◆ On one crossing in 1959 the *Queen Elizabeth* sailed to
  America with only 70 passengers and returned with
  only 130.

By the 1960s Cunard and P & O had to admit the demise of the ocean
liner and both companies turned to cruising as a new market. In Chapter
Ten we shall study the development of cruising in more detail, right from
the conversion of these ocean liners, to the modern **fly/cruise** holidays
using purpose-built cruise ships.

Politics and Tourism

The worldwide tourism scene is always changing and one of the reasons for this is that political situations in the world are constantly changing and evolving. The case of the Republic of Ireland illustrates this point well.

In 1960 the cities and towns of the Republic of Ireland were filled with small hotels and guest houses. Ferries sailed from Liverpool to Dublin daily and were invariably filled to capacity in the summer. A holiday in the Republic of Ireland was cheap, reliable, close to home and yet that little bit different with a touch of the blarney. However, once the troubles in Northern Ireland hit the headlines, the tourist trade was lost virtually overnight in the south. There were no bombs in Dublin, yet it became increasingly difficult to convince an Englishman that he would be safe in the Republic of Ireland. Finally in 1990, just 170 years after the ferry service started, the last boat the *Earl William* sailed out of Liverpool for Dublin.

Some political situations are reflected in the **visa** and entry requirements for a country. For example:

♦ Although Israel does not prohibit the entry of holidaymakers from other countries, many Arab States, who object to the Israeli treatment of Palestinians, will not allow Israelis to enter their country.

♦ Bahrain and Algeria will not allow those holding Israeli passports to enter the country.

♦ Iraq, Syria and Jordan refuse entry even to those who have an Israeli visa stamped in their passports.

A person who holds a British passport and wishes to visit Israel and then Jordan would in fact be advised to take two passports with them. In this way the Israeli visa could be in one passport and the Jordanian visa in the other.

These are some other examples of how political situations affect tourism.

♦ South Africa does not forbid any other nationalities to holiday there, but most other African states will not allow white South Africans into their country.

♦ Nigeria and Tunisia will not grant visas to white South Africans and other countries as far apart as Bulgaria, Trinidad and Tobago have similar restrictions because of their disapproval of the apartheid policy in South Africa.

♦ Australia refuses entry to any sporting teams from South Africa or indeed any individual sports person representing South Africa.

Travel agents should not assume that everyone who books a holiday through them holds a British passport. Persons who hold other nationalities are not subject to the same rules and regulations as regards visa and entry requirements. To exercise their role of giving sound advice, the travel agent would do well to ask whether the client holds a British passport if they are booking a visit to a country which has particular restrictions. These details can be found in reference manuals such as the *ABC Guide to International Travel* and the *Thomas Cook European Timetable*, and in computer information banks.

◇ *Activity 2.3* ◇

During this year keep cuttings from trade magazines and newspapers about any political situation abroad which might possibly affect tourism.

It may only start with a small incident but if you follow the story you could see if it develops into a situation such as that in Sri Lanka when British tourists were warned not to visit the country in 1989.

Mount your cuttings on blank paper and keep them in a ring binder file so that you can easily add to your collection about each country or situation.

Who Benefits from Tourism?

One view of the benefits of tourism is that visitors spend money in the host country and this money spreads quickly into the hands and the pockets of the local people.

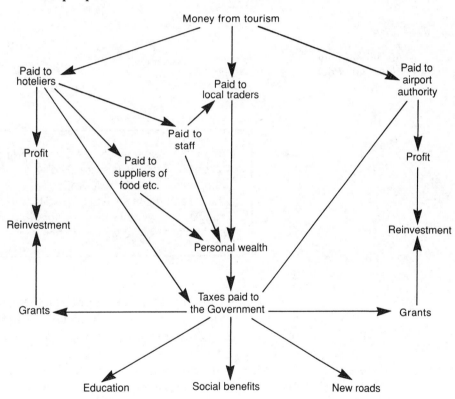

Diagram 2.2 The multiplier effect

Tourists' money goes to hotel and restaurant owners, room service staff, hairdressers and traders. The hotelier uses some of the money to buy food for guests and to pay the wages of the cooks and maids. The hotel workers spend money in the local shops, as well as paying taxes to the government. The government uses the money to provide services for the whole community. The money is therefore spread throughout the country.

This is generally referred to as the **multiplier effect** because it conjures up a picture of the money being increased and circulated throughout the country for the good of everyone.

However there is another view of the benefits of tourism which says that in some situations this is just an illusion, and that in reality most of the money **leaks out** of the host country, especially if it is a poor nation.

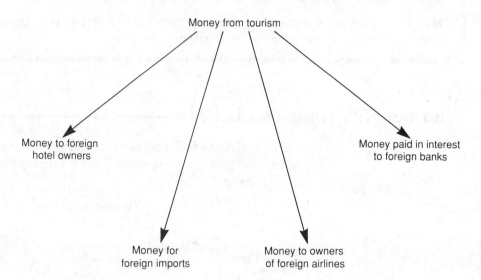

Diagram 2.3 The leakage effect

> Very often tourist hotels are owned or financed by non-nationals. Travel costs are paid to foreign airlines and companies, goods are imported especially for the tourists and these have to be paid for at a high price; and sometimes even the hotel workers and the bar-tenders are foreigners who will send their money home.

The governments of some countries have taken out loans at high interest rates in order to develop tourism in the first place, with the result that much of the money earned goes abroad to pay interest and repay the debt.

In some countries money has been invested to create roads and airports near to the tourist areas. This infrastructure does not serve the rest of the country which may have mines or fishing industries in other areas that could have benefitted from better roads and communications.

A double economy has been created, in some countries – one for the locals and another for the tourists. The presence of tourists has inflated certain prices so that, for example, it is impossible for a local person to afford to hire a beach tent, ride in a taxi cab or eat in a decent restaurant.

These are just some of the possible effects of tourism on a host country. During your educational visit to a foreign destination, use the opportunity to study the positive and negative economic, social and environmental effects of tourism on that country.

Key Events in UK Travel and Tourism

Prior to 1800:
- spa towns
- travel by coach and horses
- Grand Tour for the rich
- holy days in rural areas

1800s:
- seaside resorts
- wakes weeks
- railways
- Bank Holidays
- Thomas Cook tours

1900s:
- paid holidays
- holiday camps
- coach travel
- air travel
- charter aircraft
- tour operators
- travel agents
- cruising
- impact of tourism on host counties
- impact of politics on tourism

◇ Revision Questions ◇

1 What do you understand by the term Grand Tour?

2 What factors influenced the rapid development of Spanish resorts such as Benidorm?

3 Give five different reasons why a person might decide to take a holiday.

4 The multiplier effect on tourist money is thought to be beneficial to the economy of host countries, but some money also leaks out. Give three examples of ways in which money might leak out.

5 Name two countries that a client could not visit if their passport showed that they had visited Israel.

6 Name a country in which recent political disturbances have had an adverse effect on tourism.

7 List four occupations, apart from that of a travel agent, which depend on the tourist trade in this country.

8 How would you define a tourist rather than an excursionist?

9 Name two of the early pioneers of package holidays who have given their names to present-day travel agency chains.

10 What type of tour operator is the most numerous within ABTA?

3 *Organisations within the UK Travel Industry*

By the end of this chapter you should have increased your:

- ♦ knowledge of the role of some of the varied organisations within the travel industry;
- ♦ skills in worldwide locational geography, and observation and interview techniques.

Within the UK travel industry there are various organisations with which a travel agent may interrelate. We will look at these organisations in several areas, such as:

♦ the government and airline associations, such as IATA, which are responsible for making regulations within the industry and can be sources of information for a travel agent.

♦ the voluntary organisations and marketing bodies, such as ANTOR, which can supply information about their members' activities.

♦ the professional associations, such as the ITT, which offer advice, courses and in some cases qualifications for travel agency staff.

♦ the social organisations, such as the Travel Trades Clubs, which perform a function in providing a forum for entertainment and exchange of views and ideas between members of the travel trade.

Government Organisations

Development of Tourism Act, 1969

Prior to 1969 there was no clear government policy on tourism in the UK and this often resulted in conflicting and wasteful use of resources. In 1969 the Development of Tourism Act of Parliament established:

♦ the British Tourist Authority or the BTA, which is concerned with encouraging incoming tourism from overseas visitors,

♦ the four Tourist Boards of England, Scotland, Northern Ireland and Wales which are concerned with tourism in their own national areas.

With the passing of the 1969 Act, the BTA and the National Tourist Boards were given not only guidelines, but also the power and authority to act in the name of the government and to promote British tourism with an effective voice.

The British Tourist Authority

British Tourist Authority

- The British Tourist Authority employs about 200 staff in over 20 overseas offices. These BTA offices provide information for those who are interested in visiting this country.
- A BTA office could set up workshops or educational tours to bring together British organisations and potential overseas clients.
- One BTA initiative is to help promote training in customer care for staff in the tourist industry. Their training package includes seminars, self-study packs, handbooks and videos all aimed at improving the image we offer to tourists in this country.

Such national initiatives would have been difficult to organise prior to the introduction of the 1969 Development of Tourism Act. The national tourist boards are:

- the English Tourist Board (ETB),

- the Scottish Tourist Board (STB),

- the Wales Tourist Board (WTB),

- the Northern Ireland Tourist Board (NITB).

Each Tourist Board works within its own country to encourage the provision and improvement of tourist amenities. The Tourist Boards were empowered by the 1969 Act to promote publicity and advertising; to offer information services; to undertake research; and to provide grants for tourist related projects. The English Tourist Board, along with the British Tourist Authority, reports to the Department of Employment. The Scottish and Wales Tourist Boards are responsible to their respective Secretaries of State.

In order to extend their influence within their countries, the National Tourist Boards have set up Regional Tourist Boards.

- In England there are twelve Regional Tourist Boards.
- In Scotland there are thirty-two Regional Tourist Boards.
- In Wales there are three Regional Councils.

The tourist boards provide Tourist Information Centres (TIC) and offer a variety of publications giving details of places of interest, as well as accommodation.

*Southport Tourist
Information Centre*

Each board also participates in exhibitions and workshops and in fact the largest stand at the World Travel Market in London each year is taken by the British Tourist Authority and the National and Regional Tourist Boards. Every year the boards produce statistical facts, such as the number of visitors to particular attractions in their area, and undertake surveys and research to constantly update their information. The addresses of the National Tourist Boards are given in Chapter Four and you could write to them for up-to-date information.

◇ *Activity 3.1* ◇

Make a visit to a local tourist attraction. It may be a leisure complex, an industrial heritage museum or a shopping complex such as St Katherine's Dock in London or the Albert Dock in Liverpool.

During your visit, interview some of the visitors to the attraction. Try to talk to people who are:

a) from the local area,
b) from other parts of the United Kingdom,
c) from abroad.

Ask these people why they have come to the attraction and how often they come. Use the opportunity to discuss local tourism and its impact.

Now approach an official of the attraction – you may wish to arrange an interview in advance. With the guide or official, try to establish the history of the attraction and what funding, if any, came from the National Tourist Board, the local council or private enterprise.

Local Government and Tourism

Local government has a role to play in providing tourism and leisure facilities both for local people and for visitors to the area.

> Local councils provide leisure facilities such as swimming pools, theatres, museums, and parks. Sometimes these prove to be attractive to visitors, as is the case with the swimming centre at Rhyl in North Wales.

In Bradford, the local council made a deliberate attempt to attract tourists to the area. Staff were taken on to promote the tourist possibilities of local associations with both industrial heritage and television series such as *Emmerdale Farm* and *Last of The Summer Wine*. A subsidy was given to help open the new National Museum of Photography and the council took the initiative in providing publicity material and training for information staff and guides.

Bradford attractions

Salts Mill

Gallery Saltaire

National Museum of Photography, Film and Television

Local councils are also responsible for providing services such as litter bins, toilets and car and coach parking. Primarily these services are provided for the local people who have elected the council but, particularly in tourist centres and seaside resorts, the council will take into account the needs of visitors. In some instances, local government works with the private sector to promote a tourist attraction. In such cases the local government has to consider the interests of both the local residents and the companies who wish to develop the facilities. Even in cases where they are not collaborating with the private sector, local government usually has a role to play in that its permission has to be sought for any building or development in the area. The degree to which local councils work with their local tourist board varies throughout the country.

◊ *Activity 3.2* ◊

We can call tourism funded by national or local government the **public sector**, and tourism funded by individuals or companies the **private sector**.

Copy and complete the table below adding more examples.

	Public sector	**Private sector**
Getting there	Passport Office	Travel Agent
Leisure facilities	Local swimming Pool	Alton Towers
Entertainment	South Bank Complex	London Palladium

English Heritage

English Heritage or to give it its full title, the Historic Buildings and Monuments Commission for England, is under the directorship of the Department of the Environment. English Heritage was founded as a separate entity in 1984 to encourage public participation and interest in the many historical sites owned and operated by the government. Membership of English Heritage allows free entrance into properties ranging from castles to houses and from prehistoric sites, such as Stonehenge, to Roman remains. Free admission to the London attractions of Hampton Court Palace and the Tower of London would more than compensate for the membership fee for a family. Members of English Heritage are offered half-price admission to historic sites in Wales and

Scotland. The *English Heritage Magazine*, which is produced quarterly, keeps members up-to-date with special activities and events, as well as encouraging interest in the heritage of the country.

Stonehenge

Airline Associations

IATA

In 1945 the International Air Transport Association (IATA) was formed. IATA is a voluntary association with members from over 80 per cent of the world's airlines. The main function of IATA is to promote safe, regular and economic air transport. IATA member airlines will only pay commission to approved sales agents and this is one of the most sought after franchises for travel agents.

The **travel agent** must show the airline that the staff are trained to issue international tickets and that the business and premises are secure. Once approved, such agents can keep stocks of tickets for which they are responsible.

IATA acts as a clearing house for any disputes which might arise amongst its members. IATA was also responsible for standardising operating procedures and ticketing. Thus, passengers can now book and complete quite complicated international journeys secure in the knowledge that their ticket will be valid and acceptable worldwide.

The IATA framework has also been used for fixing fares on some international routes, although the final approval is always that of the government of the country involved. If fares are agreed, then there is less likelihood of undercutting and saving at the expense of safety. On the other hand, if prices are fixed then competition has to be on ephemeral aspects such as the design of the stewards' uniforms or the free gifts that can be given in flight. It should also be remembered that IATA members always face true financial competition from non-members. Since 1979 there has been a two-tier membership, with the fare fixing being voluntary

It is mainly the US carriers which have elected to take trade membership only.

IATA functions through its three Traffic Conference Areas of the world:

♦ TCA1 comprises North and South America,

♦ TCA2 covers Europe and Africa,

♦ TCA3 is Asia.

These are general guidelines and Activity 3.3 below will help you to get to know the areas a little better.

◊ *Activity 3.3* ◊

Using an atlas and the pink world map in an *ABC World Airways Guide* list five countries in each of the Traffic Conference Areas. Try to make these less well-known countries to extend your knowledge.

CAA

As mentioned above, it is the responsibility of governments to approve the activities of their own airlines. In Britain the approval and licensing of air carriers is the responsibility of the Civil Aviation Authority (CAA). The Civil Aviation Authority was set up by an Act of Parliament in 1971 and its principal responsibility is for the economic and safe regulation of British civil aircraft. British tour operators who sell package holidays which include charter flights are required to obtain from the CAA an Air Travel Organiser's Licence or ATOL. Those who hold an ATOL are examined each year by the CAA to ensure that they are fit to continue to hold the licence.

All ATOL holders must lodge a **bond**, which operates like an insurance for the benefit of passengers should the business fail. This bond is in addition to the bond which the company would almost certainly have with ABTA. If you look on a booking form for any of the well-known tour operators which use charter flights, you will see their ATOL number next to the logo, published for the information of their clients.

The CAA and the Ministry of Defence are jointly responsible for the National Air Traffic Service which controls flight paths over the United Kingdom. The airspace is divided into two regions with the Southern, or London, Control based at West Drayton in Middlesex, and the Northern, or Scottish, Control based at Prestwick in Ayrshire. Prestwick also has the Oceanic Area Control Centre which looks after air traffic on the busy routes to and from North America.

OCEAN CONTROL AREA

Scottish terminal control area

Prestwick

SCOTTISH FLIGHT INFORMATION REGION

Belfast control area

LONDON FLIGHT INFORMATION REGION

Isle of Man control zone

Manchester control area

Daventry control area

Birmingham control zone

London terminal control area

West Drayton

Worthing control area

0   50   100 miles

Channel Islands control zone

Diagram 3.1 Map showing UK airspaces

Congestion on the air traffic flight paths can cause problems for holidaymakers. Charter flights in particular can be affected by delays because would-be passengers have to wait at airports until their particular flight can depart. **Scheduled flight** passengers on the other hand are sometimes less affected because they can be more easily accommodated on alternative flights going to the same destination.

BAA **B·A·A**

London's Gatwick Airport is the second busiest international airport in the world and handles over 20 million passengers a year, many of them package holidaymakers on charter flights.

Gatwick Airport is owned and operated by the British Airports Authority plc (BAA). Other BAA plc airports are Heathrow and Stansted in the London area, and Glasgow, Edinburgh, Prestwick and Aberdeen in Scotland.

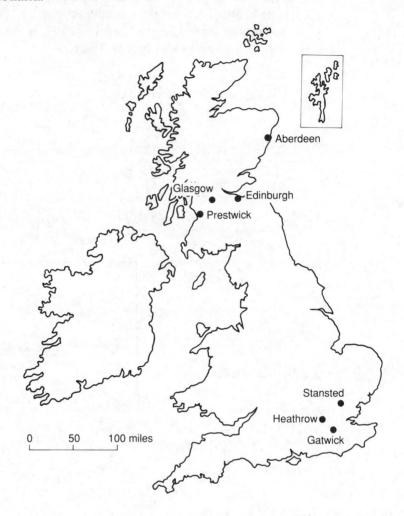

Diagram 3.2 Map showing BAA airports

Voluntary Organisations

National Trust

Despite its name, the National Trust is not a government agency but an independent charity. The National Trust was founded in 1895 by a Victorian group which included the writer Beatrix Potter. With over 1.6 million members, the National Trust is the world's largest heritage conservation charity. In the beginning, the National Trust's first concern was to preserve the countryside from the advances of the Industrial Revolution. As time went on however, the Trust also became involved with historical properties, so much so, that nowadays many people only associate the National Trust with stately homes. The National Trust extended its interest to the coastline of Britain with the special promotion of 'Enterprise Neptune'.

The National Trust produces an excellent range of leaflets on a variety of subjects such as stately homes, the preservation of the countryside, education of young people and access to sites and properties for the disabled. The address at which to contact the Trust is:

The National Trust
36 Queen Anne's Gate
London SW1H 9AS

Travel Trade Marketing Associations

Travel trade marketing associations exist to promote their own interests and travel agents should be aware of the wealth of specialist knowledge available to them through these channels.

ANTOR

association of national tourist office representatives in Great Britain.

The Association of National Tourist Office Representatives in the United Kingdom or ANTOR is a voluntary non-political organisation which represents over 80 national tourist offices from all over the world. It helps to promote the exchange of views amongst its members and within the travel industry and can bring a truly international approach to problems within the industry.

Some examples of non-British national tourist offices which are members of ANTOR are:

♦ Australian Tourist Commission,

♦ Danish NTO,

♦ Ontario Tourism,

♦ Spanish NTO,

♦ Tunisian NTO,

♦ USTTA (United States Travel and Tourism Association).

Members of ANTOR provide information about destinations within their countries and ANTOR produces a World Travel Guide each year.

ANTOR in the UK is a member of the International ANTOR Commission (IAC) which was founded in 1981. Further information about the current members and activities of ANTOR can be obtained from their headquarters at:

ANTOR
42D Compayne Gardens
London NW6 3RY

BITOA

The British Incoming Tour Operators Association, or BITOA, was founded in 1977 and represents the interests of tour operators who provide holidays, tours or tourism services for visitors coming into the United Kingdom from overseas. BITOA provides opportunities for its members:

♦ to exchange ideas and information,

♦ to develop and uphold an accepted code of conduct

♦ and to speak with a corporate voice on matters of common interest.

According to BITOA's own figures there are over 400 businesses in this country which are concerned with incoming tourism, of which about 100 are members of BITOA. BITOA members are concerned with the quality of tourism in the United Kingdom and in order to become a member of the association each company must be sponsored by two existing members who are satisfied that the new company is prepared to function in a professional manner in promoting British tourism. Further information can be obtained from the Secretariat at:

BITOA Secretariat
77 Oxford Street
London W1R 1RB

PATA

The Pacific Asia Travel Association, or PATA, was founded in Hawaii in 1952 to facilitate and promote tourism in Asia and the Pacific area. Geographically this area extends from India in the east to North America on the west of the Pacific, and from Japan and the USSR in the north to Australia and New Zealand in the south.

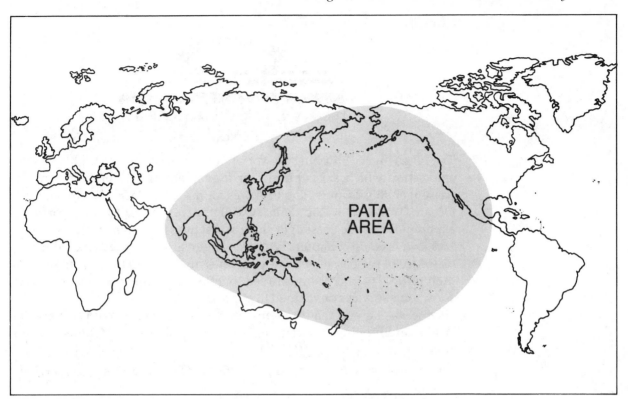

PATA membership is open to any organisation which has tourist connections in the defined area and currently there are over 2000 members. PATA members are from all sectors of the travel industry with representation from:

♦ governments,

♦ tourism bodies,

♦ airlines,

♦ shipping lines,

♦ hotel operators,

♦ and travel agencies.

PATA organises promotional activities; provides research and information services; and will give advice on tourism development within its area. In promoting tourism in Asia and the Pacific, PATA targets the main generating markets of Japan, Europe, North America and Australia. The theme of quality is emphasised with PATA's slogan 'The Pacific Asia Area – The Quality Destination'. The success of PATA in attracting the mass market to the Far East can be judged by the fact that in 1986, thirty of PATA's thirty-five member countries received over 30 million visitor arrivals for the first time. Further information can be obtained from the Secretariat of the United Kingdom Chapter at:

PATA
Box 43
Welwyn Garden City
Hertfordshire AL8 6PQ

PSA

The Passenger Shipping Association, or PSA, is a trade owners' association which exists purely for the benefit of its members, who are passenger ship owners. The PSA was founded in 1958 under the name of Ocean Travel Development (OTD) in response to the challenge experienced by the passenger ships at that time from the new jet airlines.

As we saw in Chapter Two, the larger aircraft threatened the very existence of the passenger shipping lines in 1958, and those who saw that their future lay in cruising banded together in the new association. Later, as car ferry services developed in importance, they too joined OTD until in 1976 it was agreed that the name of the association should become the Passenger Shipping Association. The primary objectives of the association are:

♦ to liaise with the government and ABTA in protecting members' interests;

♦ to promote travel agency support services.

In 1987 the PSA formed an educational arm, PSARA, or the Passenger Shipping Association Retail Agent Scheme. The PSARA scheme is open to all ABTA travel agents and aims to educate staff to sell cruising effectively.

PSARA offers a cruise manual and a comprehensive training programme with seminars, at management and assistant level, and ships' visits and familiarisation programmes. *Get Cruise Wise* the PSARA quarterly magazine offers up-to-date information and advice as well as reduced rate cruise holidays for agents.

The PSA has set up a dispute settlement procedure for cases involving car ferry based package holidays and cruises with shipping companies belonging to the association. The dissatisfied client and the company involved are asked to present their case in a written form and the PSA conciliator advises a suggested solution. If a decision cannot be agreed, the PSA can make arrangements for an independent arbitrator to consider the case.

The headquarters of the Passenger Shipping Association are at:

PSA
9/10 Market Place
London W1N 7AG

Professional Associations

ABTA

The Association of British Travel Agents, or ABTA, was founded in 1950 in response for a need for travel agents in this country to support each other in a new and growing industry. Since that time we have seen a great improvement in living standards and with it an explosion in the number of people who want to take foreign holidays. Add to this the extra capacity available since the introduction of wide bodied jets and it is understandable that travel agents and tour operators too have flourished in the last twenty or thirty years. Worldwide tourism has been one of the fastest growing industries this century.

ABTA is a self-regulatory, independent association drawing its members from both travel agents and tour operators. Over the years, ABTA has developed a dual role with responsibilities to the public, as well as to its members.

ABTA's responsibilities to the public have often caused it problems because, by the very nature of the tourist trade, the customer pays in advance for what amounts to a dream – and sometimes the reality, if not actually a nightmare, does not match up to expectations.

When things go wrong it usually means unacceptable social problems for the customer as well as damage to the reputation of the travel agent or tour operator. The customer may be affected either financially or emotionally by having to endure an excessive flight delay or dirty, unpleasant hotel accommodation. In order to protect both the public and its members, ABTA has devised:

- the Travel Agents' Code of Practice,
- the Tour Operators' Code of Practice,
- the ABTA Conciliation Scheme,
- the ABTA Arbitration Scheme.

Members of ABTA have to abide by the rules of the association or face fines or even expulsion.

The rules of the Travel Agents' Code of Practice demand that a travel agency has at least one qualified assistant who has had more than two years experience of dealing with the public in a travel agency.

The Tour Operators' Code of Practice details minimum standards for brochures, booking conditions and cancellation procedures.

The ABTA Codes of Conduct will be studied in more detail in Chapter Nine. Up-to-date copies of the Codes of Conduct can be obtained from:

ABTA Headquarters
55–57 Newman Street
London WIP 4AH

ABTA members must put up bonds, a type of insurance taken out by the company, possibly with a bank, to cover costs of repatriating, or bringing home, clients or compensating them should the company cease trading. All ABTA members agree to what is commonly referred to as **stabiliser**. 'Stabiliser' states that, with regard to foreign package holidays, ABTA travel agents should only deal with ABTA tour operators, and vice versa.

This is a restrictive practice and as such was referred to the Office of Fair Trading in 1976. The OFT took six years to decide that the practice could continue because it was thought to be in the interest of the public. This is because most travel agents and tour operators do, in fact, belong to ABTA and so the association is in a strong position to protect a wide section of the travelling public if all its members abide by the rules.

The ABTA Conciliation Scheme is a free service offered to clients who have a complaint about an ABTA member. Both the client and the company are required to put their case in writing and ABTA will recommend a decision.

The ABTA Arbitration Scheme exists for those who are not satisfied with ABTA's decision in a dispute. If the case is taken to arbitration, both the client and the company must agree to abide by the decision of the arbitrator. The case cannot be taken to court later.

To assist with training in the travel industry, ABTA has set up its National Training Board (ABTA NTB) which is responsible for organising and monitoring the ABTA Youth Training Scheme, collaborating with BTEC in producing the BTEC National Course in Travel and Tourism, as well as working with City and Guilds to create such courses as COTAC (Certificate of Travel Agency Competence) and the ABTA/City and Guilds 499 Certificate in Travel Studies.

ITT

The Institute of Travel and Tourism, or the ITT, is a professional association concerned with educational standards for both travel agents and tour operators. Its declared aim is 'to develop the professionalism of its members within the industry'. The ITT has a structured membership with non-corporate grades of students and affiliated members, and corporate grades of members who have voting rights. Corporate members are entitled to place letters after their name:

♦ A.Inst.T.T. stands for Associate Membership and holders must have reached COTAC Level II or have similar qualifications.

♦ M.Inst.T.T. stands for Full Membership and holders must have five years experience in the travel industry, plus a qualification such as a relevant degree, COTAM (Certificate of Travel Agency Management), the Institute's Examination or have presented a thesis on a travel related topic.

♦ F.Inst.T.T. stands for Fellowship and holders must have ten years experience in the travel trade or have taken the Institute Examination at Fellowship level.

♦ Honorary Fellowship can be granted by invitation only.

Each year the ITT organises seminars at several venues throughout the United Kingdom on topics which are of current interest or concern in the industry. Annually an ITT overseas study conference provides opportunities for discussion, debates, excursions and relaxation. The ITT journal is published four times a year and provides a forum for informative articles and an exchange of views. Further information about membership or the seminars for the current year can be obtained from:

ITT
113 Victoria Street
St Albans
Herts AL1 3TJ

Travel Trade Social Organisations

In general, people in the travel trade are sociable, outgoing individuals and it is not surprising to find flourishing social groups offering get-togethers and reduced rate holidays to their members.

TTC

The Travel Trades Club has representation in most regions of the country. The Regional Clubs organise sponsored events for members on a monthly basis, where normally there will be a free or reduced rate buffet, a talk or film show from the sponsor, followed by a disco or social event. Regional Clubs also have quiz evenings, some of which are contested at national level, and there is at least one reduced rate holiday for members each year. Such events are an excellent way of getting to know people within the industry in your region and many Travel Trades Clubs welcome students as temporary members.

Skal Clubs

The Association Internationale des Skal Clubs exists to promote friendship and mutual understanding among its members. There are over 500 Clubs throughout the world with a total membership of over 26 000. As membership is restricted to those who have held a position of responsibility in the travel trade for at least five years, members are normally drawn from the management level of the industry. Normally only one Skal Club can be founded in a city or municipal area and that Club will arrange monthly luncheons or dinners at which members are actually forbidden to discuss their business affairs.

◇ *Revision Questions* ◇

1 To which organisation should a tour operator apply for an ATOL?

2 a) Give the popular name for the Historic Buildings and Monuments Commission for England.
 b) Name three buildings or monuments under the Commission's care.

3 Name two types of companies which might apply for membership of ABTA.

4 Give two objectives of the National Trust.

5 State the *full name* of the organisations described below:
 a) The group within ABTA which is responsible for training travel agents.
 b) An organisation which is empowered to speak with a corporate voice on matters of common interest to companies which deal with visitors coming to the UK from overseas.
 c) An international association of over 80 airlines whose aim is to promote safe, regular and economic air transport.
 d) An educational body which is devoted to training travel agents to sell cruising effectively.
 e) An organisation which promotes tourism in over 30 Far Eastern countries.
 f) An organisation which represents the tourist interests of over 80 countries in the UK.

6 If by 'target market', we understand the people whom an organisation hopes to attract, what are the target markets of the following:
a) the ETB,
b) the BTA?

7 Name two travel trade social bodies which are organised on a national basis in this country.

8 To which government agency is the Scottish Tourist Board responsible?

9 Name four tourism or leisure facilities which could be provided by a local council in a seaside resort.

10 a) Name the company which owns and operates Heathrow Airport.
b) Name three other airports which are owned by the same company.

4 *UK Travel Geography*

By the end of this chapter you should have increased your:

- ♦ knowledge of the transport network in the UK and the variety of attractions available to tourists;
- ♦ skills in using mileage charts, measuring mileage on maps and calculating journey times for itineraries.

This chapter and the next two are concerned with travel geography, that is the location of tourist attractions and how to get there. It is impossible to cover all aspects and places of interest in these chapters, but they will serve as guidelines to help you to be more aware of the principal places of interest, as well as helping you to develop a method for studying travel geography. One of the main sources of information for the UK is the network of Tourist Information Centres throughout the country. These TICs are the responsibility of the Regional and National Tourist Boards. The addresses of the four National Tourist Board Offices and that for London are given on the next page.

Wherever you live in the country you should have a special awareness and knowledge of the capital. Many clients will want to visit London for short breaks and others will have occasion to travel through the capital. In either case you would do well to have enough information to be able to advise them about routes, accommodation and places of interest.

An awareness of your local area can be extended to other parts of the country as your interest grows. During the course you should aim to build up a file of information and you could start your own personal file by writing to these Tourist Boards:

◆ English Tourist Board
Thames Tower
Black's Road
London W6 9EL

◆ Wales Tourist Board
Brunel House
2 Fitzalan Road
Cardiff CF2 1UY

◆ London Tourist Board
26 Grosvenor Gardens
London SW1W 0DU

◆ Northern Ireland Tourist Board
River House
48 High Street
Belfast BT1 2DS

◆ Scottish Tourist Board
23 Ravelston Terrace
Edinburgh EH4 3EU

According to the BTA the top ten tourist attractions in England are:

1 British Museum, London;

2 National Gallery, London;

3 Madame Tussaud's, London;

4 Alton Towers, Staffordshire;

5 Science Museum, London;

6 Tower of London;

7 Tate Gallery, London;

8 Blackpool Tower;

9 Natural History Museum, London;

10 London Zoo.

The statistics for this league table are based on the number of visitors to the centres in a year. Attractions which are missing from this list are the natural ones such as:

◆ the Lake District,

◆ the New Forest,

◆ the Highlands of Scotland.

These are missing from the list because of the nature of the statistics, which are collected as people pay at the turnstiles to enter the man-made attractions of the top ten. Areas of natural beauty around the country are freely open to anyone and some of them are actively preserved as National Parks or through the work of the National Trust.

In this chapter, after considering some basic information, both natural and man-made attractions will be highlighted.

◊   *Activity 4.1*   ◊

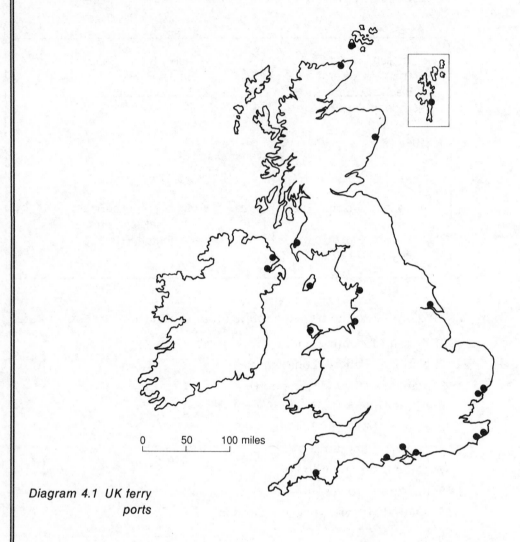

*Diagram 4.1 UK ferry
ports*

Copy the map in Diagram 4.1 above and, with the help of an atlas, fill in the following information:

1 Draw in the borders between England, Wales, Scotland and Northern Ireland.

2 Mark and name London, Cardiff, Edinburgh, and Belfast.

3 The twenty dots on the map indicate ferry ports. Make a collection of current ferry brochures and use them to name the ports on the map.

4 With the aid of an AA manual or any other suitable reference material, mark the motorways of England, Wales and Scotland.

5 Using the atlas or other suitable reference material, mark the following airports on your map – London (Heathrow, Gatwick, Stansted), Luton, Birmingham, Manchester, Leeds/ Bradford, Newcastle, Cardiff, Glasgow.

6 Obtain a map of InterCity rail routes, from the local BR Information Service.

7 Obtain a map of Rapide bus routes, from the local National Express Information Service.

Itineraries

In order to work efficiently in a travel agency, you will need to be able to give information on what to see and how to get there. It is equally important to be able to give some indication to a client as to how long it will take to reach a destination. Maps and mileage charts are used to find out the distances between places. The time taken to cover the distance will then depend on the speed at which the person is travelling.

When calculating the times involved for a journey,

♦ first estimate the distance, then

♦ estimate the time to travel by dividing the mileage, or distance, by the average speed, and

♦ suggest a break in the journey every two hours or every 100 miles, whichever is more convenient.

Mileage charts can be found in atlases, guide books and even diaries.

Diagram 4.2 shows a simple version of a mileage chart which appears as a triangle.

MILEAGE CHART

Aberdeen	Aberdeen											
Birmingham	405	Birmingham										
Cambridge	446	100	Cambridge									
Dover	559	182	112	Dover								
Exeter	559	162	218	242	Exeter							
Glasgow	142	287	350	463	441	Glasgow						
Hull	341	124	123	236	279	245	Hull					
Leicester	412	39	68	169	191	299	87	Leicester				
Manchester	329	79	154	255	235	211	93	87	Manchester			
Oxford	466	64	80	129	138	350	156	69	142	Oxford		
Perth	81	329	371	484	484	61	265	322	254	390	Perth	
York	303	127	151	264	289	207	38	103	64	172	228	York
London	492	110	54	72	170	392	168	98	184	57	417	196	London

Diagram 4.2

To find the appropriate mileage:

♦ find the place you are leaving down the left hand side;

♦ find the place you are going to along the slope;

♦ once you have found both places, use your finger or a ruler to trace across the line from the left hand name until you are directly under the other name;

♦ the number you have reached will give the mileage between the two places.

If you wish to travel from Manchester to Hull, you locate Manchester down the left hand side and then move across reading the numbers 329, 79, 154, 255, 235, 211, until you reach 93 for Hull.

Some mileage charts give the distances in kilometres and some will give both kilometres and miles. It is useful to remember that eight kilometres are equal to five miles. You may be asked by a client to change kilometres into miles. To do this you multiply by $\frac{5}{8}$. So:

$$40 \text{ kilometres} = \frac{40 \times 5}{8} = \frac{200}{8} = 25 \text{ miles}$$

Sometimes you may have to give an indication of distance for smaller places which are not to be found in charts. To do this you will need to be able to gauge distances on a map. Diagram 4.3 shows a simple extract from a map. You will need a sheet of paper measuring at least 30 × 21 cm and a pencil.

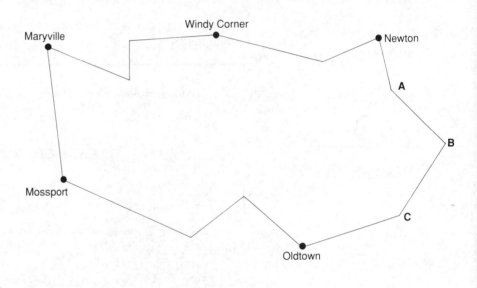

Diagram 4.3 A simple map

To estimate the distance between Newtown and Oldtown:

♦ Place a corner of the sheet of paper on the dot marking the centre of Newtown, making sure that a long edge lies on the road, until you reach point **A**.

♦ Now put the pencil tip down firmly at this point on the paper and swing the edge of the paper around until it is once again lying along the road.

♦ At point **B** you will again need to use the pencil as a pivot to swing the edge of the paper around on to the road.

♦ Continue in this way until you reach Oldtown and then mark the point reached on the edge of the paper.

♦ Now place the edge of the paper against the scale and read off the mileage. You will have to place it against the scale several times because the distance is greater than the 10 miles given.

Using the edge of the paper in this way you have, in fact, just stretched out the road into a straight line.

Another way of measuring distances on maps is to use a piece of string and to lay it along the route. If you start at Newtown and finish at Oldtown, when you take up the piece of string it will be the length of the road on the map. You can then read off the mileage by measuring the length of string against the scale in the same way as above. This is a simpler method than using paper and pencil but, whereas paper is usually available, balls of string are not so common! Distance calculating pens are also now available from some stationers. By tracing the line of the route on the map, with these pens, the distance covered is shown in a window at the top of the pen, either in kilometres or in miles.

Natural Attractions

Certain areas of the country have been set aside as National Parks. Diagram 4.4 shows the National Parks of England and Wales. These are good places to start if a client wishes to see an area renowned for its natural beauty.

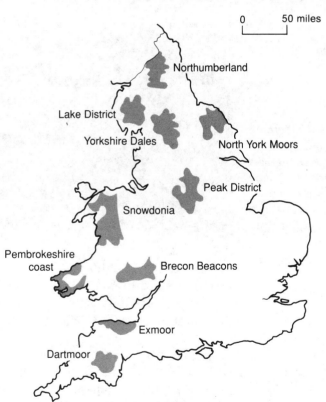

Diagram 4.4 The National Parks of England and Wales

The National Parks offer walks through varied scenery and no one could ever forget a sight such as that in the North York Moors in late summer when the ground is covered with a mass of purple heather.

A Ranger Service will guide clients through easy or medium walks in the National Parks. For the more experienced walkers there are routes such as the Cleveland Way which circles the northern edges of the North

York Moors or the 40-mile Lyke Wake Walk which crosses the moors from Osmotherley to Ravenscar.

The Lake District and the Yorkshire Dales are also very popular with motorists and it is possible to buy touring books which suggest routes to see the scenery as well as some villages off the beaten track. Clients should be encouraged to explore these areas and not to spend their time in a traffic jam on the main roads through the parks.

Snowdonia National Park covers 800 square miles and is dominated by Snowdon itself which, at 3569 ft, is the highest mountain in Wales. The scenery in the Park offers a mixture of mountains, lakes and deep valleys, and there are some noted beauty spots such as Betws-y-Coed.

The 167 mile footpath of the Pembrokeshire coast preserves the wild nature of the landscape from Amroth to St Dogmaels, near to Cardigan

The lochs and Highlands of Scotland have scenery and beauty which it would be hard to match in any part of the world.

The Northern Ireland Tourist Board produces motorists' tours taking in the winding coastline, the beautiful mountains of Mourne and the Fermanagh lakes.

The Countryside Commission has designated many places as Areas of Outstanding Natural Beauty (AONB). These areas vary in size and include mountains, fells and dales, cliffs, sand-dunes and tidal flats, as well as woods and areas preserved for wildlife. Diagram 4.5 (page 45) shows the AONB in England and Wales and the Heritage Coasts. Heritage Coasts cover some 730 miles of coastline and preserve areas of particular beauty ranging from magnificent cliffs to rolling sand-dunes.

Most of the coast of the island of Anglesey is protected as an AONB for its unspoiled beaches and bird colonies. The Cotswolds, Britain's second largest AONB, is an area of limestone hill country with attractive

Loch Lomond in Strathclyde is the largest lake in the UK but is within easy reach of Edinburgh or Glasgow.

Inverness has long been regarded as the 'Capital of the Highlands' and is the gateway to the Cairngorms, the battle-field of Culloden and Loch Ness, with its stories of monsters dating back to the seventh century.

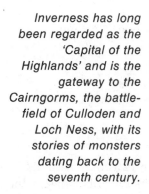

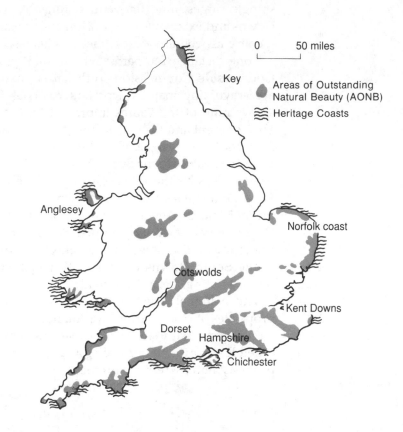

Diagram 4.5 Areas of Outstanding Natural Beauty and Heritage Coasts in England and Wales

0   50 miles

Kirk Yetholm

Pennine Way

Cleveland Way

Scarborough

Filey

Hull

Malham

Wold's Way

Prestatyn

Manchester   **Edale**

Offa's Dyke Path

Pembrokeshire Coast Path

Ridgeway Path

Monmouth

Chepstow

North Downs Way

North Devon Path   **South Downs Way**

South West Peninsula

Cornwall Coast path

Coast Path

Diagram 4.6 Long distance footpaths and bridleways in England and Wales

Cotswold-stone towns and villages. Chichester Harbour with its sea creeks and tidal flats is a yachtsman's paradise. The Norfolk Coast, which is also preserved as a Heritage Coastline, is a unique area of sand-dunes, shingle ridges, mud flats and saltings. A sixty-mile stretch of the Kent Downs and extensive areas of Dorset and Hampshire include magnificent scenery as well as some attractive villages.

Long-distance footpaths and bridleways are also designated by the Countryside Commission so that it is possible to enjoy these beautiful areas avoiding major towns and roads as far as possible. Diagram 4.6 shows nine of the routes approved by the Secretaries of State for the Environment and for Wales. The Pennine Way was the first long-distance footpath to be designated and it links three National Parks and stretches from Derbyshire to the Scottish borders. It can be walked in fourteen days, or even less by the exceptionally fit. The longest footpath is the South West Peninsula Coast Path which follows the old coastguards' paths through North Devon, Cornwall, South Devon and Dorset. The South Downs Way is the only long-distance bridleway, which means that horse-riders and cyclists as well as walkers can enjoy the path following the ridge of the South Downs in an AONB which stretches from Eastbourne to South Harting, near Petersfield.

The National Trust is the country's largest private landowner. Its properties include farms, woodland, nature reserves, 50 villages and hamlets, and many stretches of coastline. The Trust has a special campaign called Enterprise Neptune devoted to acquiring and preserving coastline property, and currently it protects 500 miles of coastline in England, Wales and Northern Ireland. There is an independent National Trust for Scotland. With concern for conservation, the National Trust controls access to its land. One way used by the National Trust to control access to its land is to limit the size of car parks. Car parks are also screened as far as possible by tree planting.

◇ *Activity 4.2* ◇

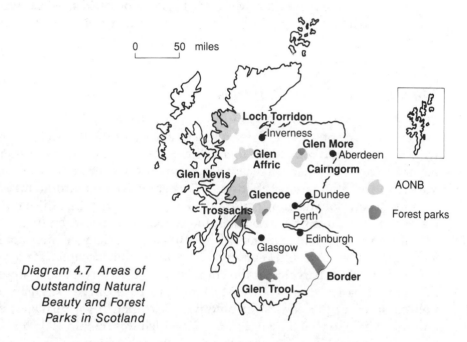

Diagram 4.7 Areas of Outstanding Natural Beauty and Forest Parks in Scotland

By now you should be building up a file of information about the UK. You have been given plenty of information about England and Wales and in this activity you will have the opportunity to extend your knowledge of Scotland. Diagram 4.7 shows AONBs and Forest Parks in Scotland.

Construct an itinerary for a Scottish touring holiday for a family of four (two adults and two children aged 11 and 13).

The tour should start and finish in Edinburgh where the family has arrived by motorail, and it should last no longer than three weeks. You may choose the time of year in which they are travelling.

Your itinerary should include a map, the route, a description of places of interest and suggested overnight stops. Your clients should be able to see a variety of scenery and places, without having to spend each night in a different hotel or guesthouse.

Useful source materials for this activity are:

♦ *'Scotland for Me'* magazines,

♦ Brochures on skiing in Scotland,

♦ Publicity material from the Scottish Regional Tourist Boards,

♦ AA books and atlases.

Man-Made Attractions

With the uncertain weather of Britain, man-made attractions are becoming ever more popular. Almost every town has a museum or an art gallery, some have zoos, others have castles, ancient abbeys or stately homes within an hour's drive. In the last few years indoor attractions have sprung up around the country. The success of theme parks such as Alton Towers and Thorpe Park depends on some of their facilities being available regardless of the weather. Exhibitions and displays connected with our industrial heritage have been brought to life with living museums such as Wigan Pier and the Ironbridge Museum. Leisure complexes, both private and municipal, can offer all-day entertainment in tropical heat under cover.

Museums and Art Galleries

Throughout the country we are fortunate to have a wide network of museums, many of which are free to the public. From the British Museum with its worldwide reputation to small local collections, most museums have changed their image in recent years and the dour curator has become the friend and confidante of children as they enter a new environment.

In the Liverpool Museum, children queue to be the first into the natural history section during afternoons in the school holidays when there are countless activities and exhibits for them to use. The Science Museum in Kensington, London could keep anyone, child or adult, occupied for days.

One of the best bargains in the country must be the National Railway Museum, a part of the Science Museum, but based in York. Here are housed some of the earliest locomotives; Victorian royal carriages; an enormous engine weighing over 190 tons which was built in 1935 for the Chinese National Railway; and many more, including *Mallard*, which holds the world speed record for steam locomotives.

> York also has the country's largest folk museum in the Castle Museum. This collection was started by a country doctor at the end of the last century as he made his round of visits and saw a traditional way of life that was still unaffected by the modern world. He began to collect items of interest, many of which other people regarded as mere rubbish. His collection extended from truncheons, bicycles and musical boxes to fireplaces, redundant farm equipment and even shop fronts. Today it is possible to walk down cobbled streets within the museum, to enter shops which have the sights and smells of Victorian days, and even, bringing heritage nearer to our own day, to see a fully fitted sitting room and kitchen of the 1950s.

In your own area there will be museums and art galleries so try to find out what they have to offer, especially in the way of promotions during holiday times.

Historical Buildings and Country Houses

Historical buildings such as cathedrals, abbeys and castles hold a special fascination for some people, especially for overseas visitors who want to capture the spirit of our culture. The Department of the Environment under the banner of English Heritage operates many of these properties. For example, Fountains Abbey in Yorkshire is said to be one of the finest examples in Europe of a mediaeval monastery. Much of it is now in ruins but it is still possible to trace the life of the monastic community who lived there.

Many British cities have magnificent cathedrals, such as York, Winchester, Salisbury and the post war cathedral at Coventry.

In Wales there are castles dating from the earliest times to the series of castles built or strengthened by Edward I in the late thirteenth and early fourteenth centuries. The beautiful Caernarfon Castle was the scene for the investiture of the Prince of Wales and is one of Britain's best known historical sites. Chepstow Castle which stands in a superb setting above the Wye river was probably the first stone castle in Britain. New parts were added to the original castle right up to the Civil War, and so it illustrates different periods of castle building.

Britain is rich in country houses which are not only furnished in their period style but have been lived in by the same family for generations. Indeed in some of the smaller properties it is possible to chat with the owners. Privately owned homes sometimes specialise in topics which are of interest to their owner. One such is Arley Hall in Cheshire which has spectacular gardens and also encourages local craftsmen to demonstrate their skills for visitors.

Many stately home owners have realised that they need to entertain children while parents enjoy the historical treasures and so adventure playgrounds have been introduced. The Earl of Shelburne at Bowood in Wiltshire has a paradise of treetop cabins, rope bridges, trampolines and a life size pirate galleon to delight any child.

Even the Queen opens her doors to the public at Sandringham in the summer. There are extensive car parks outside the main gate and the grounds, gardens and main house can all be visited.

The National Trust cares for a wide variety of buildings of architectural and historical interest. These range from humble cottages which may be rented to tenants, to larger houses of country families.

- The home of the Browne family at Townend, Troutbeck in the Lake District dates from the seventeenth century and contains much of the Brownes' personal furniture and belongings.

- Sizergh Castle in Cumbria was in the Strickland family from the thirteenth century until it was handed into the care of the National Trust in 1950.

- Little Moreton Hall in Cheshire is a fine example of a traditional timber-frame black and white construction.

The National Trust manages 140 country houses, some of which, like Hardwick Hall in Derbyshire, Petworth House in West Sussex and Blickling Hall in Norfolk, have great collections of art and furniture. The gardens of many of these houses are also of interest. The guide book of Blickling Hall takes the visitor through the gardens with every detail of shrubs and trees.

Industrial Heritage

In recent years industrial heritage has become a popular subject for tourism. Buildings dating from the industrial revolution have been restored and tools and implements associated with the local trades are displayed in an attractive and informative manner.

In Staffordshire there is the Wrekin Heritage where, within a ten mile radius, it is possible to visit the Aerospace Museum at RAF Cosford, the Ironbridge Gorge Museum and the Midland Motor Museum as well as the Severn Valley Railway. Ironbridge, which claims to be the birthplace of the Industrial Revolution, has a total of six museum sites for the visitor. Wigan in Lancashire has capitalised on an old music-hall joke and created Wigan Pier, a unique complex of restored canalside warehouses and mill buildings. However this is no dry museum for within its walls you can enter the living world of cloggers, tinsmiths and boltmakers; you can become a child again in a real life Victorian schoolroom, complete with the strictest of teachers; and you can even pay your respects in a bereaved home where you are welcomed through the kitchen by the son of the house.

The accidental discovery of Viking remains on the building site for a supermarket led eventually to the fascinating Jorvik Museum in York. At Jorvik you can travel backwards in a time carriage and wander through the main street of Viking York, complete with realistic sights, sound and even smells. At the end of the tour, for the Viking enthusiast, there is a museum of actual treasure found on the site during the excavations. The prize exhibit is the Coppergate Helmet, which is not Viking but is in fact a unique example of the kind of helmet probably worn by royal or noble Anglo-Saxons in Northumbria at about the time of the first Viking attacks.

The same company which created this unusual museum has gone on to create equally fascinating historical exhibitions at Canterbury and Oxford.

Wigan Pier

Theme Parks

Theme parks hold great attraction for all ages in all parts of the country. These parks usually have fairground rides for children, teenagers and adults alike. Many have beautiful gardens, and all aim to provide enough undercover entertainment to keep clients happy for at least one full day.

Thorpe Park in Surrey is accessible to clients in the Greater London area and each summer has over a million visitors. The organisers claim that there are up to four hours of entertainment completely undercover should the weather be bad.

- ◆ Alton Towers, in Staffordshire, is very centrally located for clients from most parts of England and Wales, and its popularity testifies to this. It not only contains a fairground to rival any other for youngsters, but its gardens are also a pleasure for more sedate clients.

- ◆ The American Adventure in Derbyshire and the Magical Kingdom of Camelot in Lancashire, while not on the same scale as the other parks, nevertheless offer great days out, with undercover entertainment and thrilling and daring rides.

- ◆ Granada Studios in Manchester is a new style of theme park which takes the visitor into the magical world of television where everything is not what it seems. You can walk down famous streets, drink in famous bars, become a child in a giant's world or chat with the housekeeper of Sherlock Holmes in his private study.

The theme parks also have an eye to the business world with each one offering conference or business entertaining facilities.

Leisure Complexes

Leisure and sports facilities are becoming very popular with today's emphasis on fitness and health. Some local authorities have opened their own facilities, such as the dry ski slope at Southampton and the Waves Water Fun Centre at Blackburn.

Holiday centres

♦ Center Parcs in Nottinghamshire, one of the largest privately owned complexes, has a central dome over the swimming area creating a subtropical paradise.

♦ Butlins holiday camps, now owned by the Rank Organisation, were totally updated during the 1980s. Five of the original camps have been renamed Holiday Worlds and the brochure also offers holidays in five hotels. The Holiday Worlds offer self-catering, half or full board accommodation. Entertainment facilities include fairgrounds, fully equipped theatres, fun pools with slides and flume rides, and clubs to occupy children of all ages.

♦ Fred Pontin started his holiday camps in the late 1940s and today's brochure offers a choice of twenty Holiday Centres around England and Wales, as well as Plemont Bay on Jersey. Five of the mainland Centres are Chalet Hotels with full table service as well as all the entertainment offered in the other centres. Five of the Pontins holiday centres offer holidays for adults only. These are very popular with older people, particularly during the summer months of the school holidays.

Diagram 4.8 Canals and Waterways of England and Wales

These leisure and holiday centres offer holidays which are very often enjoyed by three generations of a family. Some of the centres which have been built on flat land near to the sea are also particularly suitable for holidays for the disabled.

The management in most of the larger hotels throughout the country realise the attraction of these complexes and it is not uncommon to find a hotel offering not just a small swimming pool but also a jaccuzi, sauna and sunbeds together with a mini gym. Such facilities add to the potential of the hotel for staging conferences and business entertainment.

The popularity of leisure and water accounts for the rise in bookings for canal holidays in the 1980s. Diagram 4.8 shows the network of canals and waterways throughout England and Wales. It is possible to hire barges and boats in most parts of the country and travel at a leisurely pace along these networks.

◊ *Activity 4.3* ◊

Add your own suggestions to the lists below. In doing so you should try to include suggestions for your own area, for the London area and for offshore islands of the UK such as the Channel Islands and the Isle of Man.

Tourists like to go:

♦ *To the seaside* – Blackpool, Brighton, . . .
♦ *To beautiful countryside* – the Scottish Highlands, Snowdonia, . . .
♦ *To museums and art galleries* – the Tate Gallery, Manchester Museum of Science and Industry, . . .
♦ *To cathedrals, abbeys and castles* – Salisbury, Conwy Castle, Rievaulx Abbey, . . .

♦ *To stately homes* – Longleat, Blickling Hall, . . .
♦ *To theme parks* – Alton Towers, Thorpe Park, . . .
♦ *To leisure complexes* – Center Parcs, Ski-Rossendale, . . .
♦ *To shopping malls* – Covent Garden, Albert Dock, . . .
♦ *To specialist tourist attractions* – Madame Tussauds, Granada Studios, . . .
♦ *To industrial heritage and folk attractions* – Castle Museum, Wigan Pier, . . .

Your lists can be as long as you wish and you can, of course, add your own headings to this list.

◊ *Revision Questions* ◊

1 Name the county in which you would find each of the following resorts: Southport, Torquay, New Quay, Oban, Rye, Newquay, Saltcoats, Scarborough, Great Yarmouth, Rhyl.

2 Name three officially designated Areas of Outstanding National Beauty and explain how to reach them from your home town.

3 Name three English National Parks.

4 Name Birmingham's two main Intercity railway stations.

5 From which UK ports could you start the following ferry crossings?
a) England to Spain;
b) Scotland to Northern Ireland;
c) Britain to Eire;
d) Britain to Denmark;
e) Britain to Holland.

6 Name the nearest town or city to the following attractions: Jorvik Viking Centre, Stonehenge, Chatsworth, Cheddar Gorge, Petworth House, Granada Studios, Alton Towers, Fountains Abbey, Ironbridge Gorge, Madame Tussaud's Royalty and Railway Exhibition.

7 Name the motorways linking the following:
   a) Preston to Birmingham;
   b) Birmingham to Exeter;
   c) London to Bristol;
   d) Sheffield to London;
   e) London to Dover.

8 Name the city in which you would find each of the following attractions: Palace of Holyrood; Castle Museum; National Museum of Photography, Film and Television; Science Museum; National Railway Museum.

9 Name two national organisations dedicated to the preservation of the coastline and countryside in England.

10 Name three airports in the London area.

5 European Travel Geography

By the end of this chapter you should have increased your:

♦ knowledge of European locational geography with particular reference to France, Spain, Italy, Yugoslavia, Greece and the Alpine areas;

♦ skills with regard to awareness of different types of holidays and the use of brochures and reference material to find specific tourist information.

In this chapter we shall look at some of the most popular destinations for British tourists in Europe. You will need to be aware of current trends as shown in the travel trade press and daily newspapers. There are new markets opening up all the time and not only will you be giving your clients a good service by keeping abreast of trends, but you will probably find it personally and professionally interesting.

The national tourist offices and information centres which are listed in the *Travel Trade Directory*, are excellent sources of material for creating a European file of information.

The World Travel Market (WTM) is an invaluable source of information and material. The WTM is an exhibition held at Olympia in London in late November or the beginning of December each year. This is the largest travel trade show in the world and countries such as France, Spain, Portugal, Switzerland and Austria are always well represented. The World Travel Market affords an opportunity to talk to nationals from other countries, as well as being able to take away virtually as much material as you are able to carry.

In order to ascertain the relative importance for British tourists of the various European countries, make a collection of the most popular brochures on travel agents' shelves. Your collection should include standard summer, winter, skiing and city break brochures.

◇ Activity 5.1 ◇

1 You will need a map of Europe such as that in Diagram 5.1, an atlas and three coloured pencils or felt tips in blue, yellow and red.
   a) With the help of the atlas, name all the countries shown on the map.
   b) Study the city break brochures you have collected and then mark and name on your map the cities which are featured.
   c) Now colour in blue the countries which are featured in the skiing brochures.

d) Colour in yellow the countries which are in the summer brochures.

e) Finally colour in red those countries which appear in the winter brochures. If any of these have already been coloured in, use red stripes over the previous colour.

2 Some of the cities you have marked will be capitals of their countries. These are usually fascinating destinations for those who have an interest in culture and heritage. They are also important business destinations and very often have the gateway airport to a country.

With the aid of an atlas, list the places below under the correct heading of 'country' or 'capital' on a sheet of paper. Then fill in the space opposite each one with its corresponding capital or country.

France,   Madrid,   Lisbon,   Belgium,
Germany,   Berne,   Italy,   Holland,   Vienna,
Bulgaria,   Turkey,   Bucharest,   Poland,
Budapest,   Oslo,   Denmark,   Sweden,
Iceland, Valetta.

Example:

Country	Capital
France	Paris

Diagram 5.1 Europe

France

Apart from marking Paris, it is quite possible that you have only coloured parts of France blue on your map in the above activity and yet it is a very important country from the point of view of British tourism. France is very popular as a destination for British tourists who prefer to drive their own car and who want to camp or caravan or use some of the excellent and varied accommodation which is available in France.

Many brochures are more concerned with the mass tourist market of package holidays by air to destinations in Spain, Italy or Greece. The larger tour operators produce these brochures but more specialist tour operators offer smaller brochures which sometimes give the client the opportunity to put together a more personalised holiday. These brochures will offer a choice as regards:

♦ the means of travel,

♦ the route to be taken,

♦ the length of stay,

♦ the type of accommodation.

If you have not already done so, it would be useful to note the ferry crossings between England and France. You will see that there are a number of companies operating these routes. These routes vary from the shortest crossing between Dover and Calais, to the longer Plymouth to Roscoff crossing which takes clients directly to Brittany without a long drive through France.

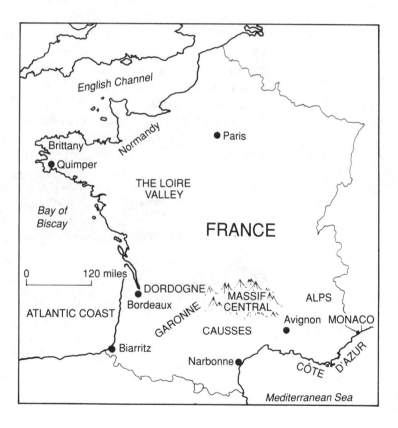

Diagram 5.2 France

Diagram 5.2 shows some of the areas of France which are popular with British tourists. Diagram 5.3 (page 58) also gives an indication of travelling times from the French ports to some of the popular areas of France. These timings are based on a car travelling at 40 miles per hour, without stops and using major roads. The timings are only given as a guideline.

	From:						
	Calais Boulogne Dunkerque	**Dieppe**	**Cherbourg**	**Le Havre**	**Caen**	**St Malo**	**Roscoff**
To: **Normandy**	5–7	3–4	1–2	2–3	1–2	1–2	3–5
Brittany	8–11	6–8	3–6	5–6	3–6	1–4	1–5
Loire Valley	8	5	5	4	4	5	7
The Causses	14	11	11	10	9	10	12
Atlantic Coast	16	12	12	13	12	10	12
Côte d'Azur	18	18	17	17	19	17	20

Diagram 5.3 Hours of travelling time from French ports

Gîtes

There is a system of self-catering accommodation called **gîtes** which are peculiar to France. Gîtes are privately owned properties, modernised with the help of the French government and supervised by the non-profit making Fédération Nationale des Gîtes. The company can be contacted through its London address at 178 Piccadilly, London W1V 0AL. A gîte may be a small cottage, a village house, a flat in a farmhouse or rooms in a château. As they can be in quiet rural areas, they afford a good opportunity for clients who wish to observe and even become part of French life and culture.

A typical gîte and the Gîtes de France symbol

Brittany

Brittany is the peninsula in northern France which juts out into the Atlantic and where the sea is never more than 50 miles away. The area has a Celtic culture distinct from the rest of France and more akin to the Celtic areas of Britain such as Cornwall, Wales and Scotland.

The many scattered fishing ports of Brittany offer quaint and interesting backdrops for the tourist, as well as being centres for yachting. The light in this northern part of France makes the ports ideal subjects for artists. Inland, there are many villages dating from the Middle Ages which have narrow winding streets of brown and cream half-timbered houses. Most villages can boast a market, and some have interesting prehistoric remains, such as the ancient standing stones at Carnac.

Quimper on the River Odet is particularly attractive to tourists during the Cornouaille Festival in July when all the local villages are represented in a fantastic parade celebrating the culture of the Breton people. The people of each village dress in their traditionally embroidered black velvet costumes and carry flowers, fishing baskets, or dogs – indeed anything that could be regarded as typical of their village. The black and white Breton flag is in great evidence and traditional instruments, such as the bagpipes, are played as the procession marches past.

Normandy

Normandy has a rugged coastline in the north which is similar to Cornwall. Inland there is beautiful woodland scenery. The coastline has associations with battles in both the First and Second World Wars and the area round Arromanches is particularly interesting to ex-soldiers and historians.

Loire Valley

The Loire Valley is a beautiful area with its gentle, soft landscape chosen by aristocrats over the centuries for their country houses. Today it is a popular area for tourists with its many châteaux open to the public, and rose nurseries, flower gardens and fruit trees which are particularly beautiful in the spring.

The Causses

The Causses in the southern part of the Massif Central has spectacular limestone plateaux and gorges, and daily living is cheap for those who are prepared to live as the French do. This is not the ideal holiday for those who expect to find Coca-Cola and hamburgers at every corner.

The Dordogne

Further west the Dordogne river flows through an area which has several other beautiful and interesting rivers and finally meets the River Garonne north of Bordeaux before emptying into the Bay of Biscay. This Atlantic Coast area of France has many smaller resorts, as yet unspoilt by mass tourism. The inland areas boast dramatic and beautiful scenery.

The French Alps

The French Alps provide one of the most important skiing areas in Europe. With the height of the Alps reaching to over 6000 feet, snow can be guaranteed even in the mildest winter. The purpose-built resorts in the Alps offer good accommodation at reasonable prices and ski runs which would test even the most proficient skier.

Côte d'Azur

The Côte d'Azur or French Riviera on the south-eastern coast of France is long established as a tourist area. Here are the world famous Nice, Cannes and further east the Principality of Monaco with its casino.

On the Côte d'Azur the beautiful, rich and famous parade themselves on their yachts and in the gambling clubs, or hide from view in their closely guarded homes. The lure and attraction of such an area is inevitable and, alongside the rich and famous, there are countless tent and caravan sites for the not-so-rich.

Transport

Most areas of France are made easily accessible for the motorist by the French Motorail system as well as the network of motorways or auto routes. The trains travel through the night from Boulogne, Dieppe or Calais to take clients and their cars to Bordeaux, Biarritz, Narbonne, Avignon or the Côte d'Azur. Passengers must book overnight sleepers and these vary from second class six-berth couchettes, in which the client can simply lie down and rest, to first class sleepers with properly made-up beds and *en suite* washing facilities.

Paris

Paris, the capital of France, has that international atmosphere which makes it special to people the world over. There are many guide books as well as specialist brochures available and you should make a special study of the attractions of Paris, both in the city and within a day's excursion trip.

Paris attractions

A project about Paris should include pictures and information about:

♦ the Eiffel Tower which dominates the Seine,

♦ the Arc de Triomphe in which the eternal flame burns,

♦ the Champs Elysées leading down to

♦ the Place de la Concorde with its Egyptian obelisk and

♦ the churches of Notre Dame and Sacré Coeur.

The list of buildings alone is endless, before you even consider the fashionable stores and numerous night clubs and shows for which Paris is so famous.

Summary for France

Capital:
Paris.

Currency:
French Franc (fr. = 100 centimes). Some hotels will change money but the most convenient places are the Credit Mutuel and the Credit Agricole which are the French equivalent of British savings banks.

Getting there:
By air – there are airports in Paris (Charles de Gaulle and Orly), Bordeaux, Lille, Lyon, Marseille, Nice and Toulouse.

By sea – English Channel ferry ports include Dunkirk, Calais, Boulogne, Dieppe, Le Havre, Caen, Cherbourg, St Malo, Roscoff. The south of France can be accessed by sea through the ports of Marseilles, Toulon and Nice.

By rail – there are connections, including the ferry crossing, from London using British Rail and the French Railway (SNCF).

Main interests for British tourists include:
The sights of Paris, the tranquility of Brittany, the sunshine of the south of France, the pleasure of touring, and skiing in the Alps.

Banking hours:
0900–1200 and 1400–1600 Monday to Friday. However while some banks close all day Saturday, others close all day Monday.

Shopping hours:
0900–1830 Monday to Saturday in the larger stores, but many stores outside Paris close for a two-hour lunch break. Hypermarkets are usually open until 2100. Small bakeries will often open on a Sunday, but may be closed on Mondays.

Special note:
In the months of July and August, when the French take their holidays, the city attractions are quieter while the coastal resorts are more crowded.

Spain

Madrid

Madrid, the capital of Spain, does not have the international jet-setting image of Paris, but nevertheless it is a fascinating city and is important as a business destination. In winter Madrid, which is on the high plateau, is very cold but in summer it is so hot that the Spanish government moves north to San Sebastian on the Atlantic coast.

Madrid has many interesting museums, the largest of which is the Prado which houses paintings by artists of the Spanish, Italian and Venetian schools as well as works of classical sculpture. The Plaza Mayor is a magnificent large Square enclosed by some of the most beautiful buildings in Europe.

The countryside surrounding Madrid is filled with castles and ancient cities.

♦ Segovia has its Alcazar, the fortress built by the Moors, as well as the long viaduct which the Romans constructed across the city.

♦ Toledo, a former capital of Spain, was world famous at one time for its swords and jewellery.

♦ The dramatic walled city of Avila is a well preserved medieval city with many historical connections.

Most British tourists who travel to Spain on a package holiday go for the sun and sand of the 'costas'. These are the areas along the Mediterranean coastline, stretching from the Costa Brava near the French border, through Barcelona and the Costa Dorada, to Benidorm and the Costa Blanca and down to the Costa de Almeria and finally the Costa del Sol on the south coast.

The Costa Brava

The Costa Brava, or the 'wild rugged coast' was the first area to open up to tourists in large numbers, with many resorts along the coastline of Catalonia.

The Costa Brava is accessible through the airport at Gerona. Most of the resorts of the Costa Brava are either small fishing villages which have been taken over by tourists, or resorts such as Malgrat which are a cluster of hotels and apartments lying along the coast and the main railway line to Barcelona.

Much of the accommodation in this area is now becoming dated but it still provides holidays at the best value for money for the average tourist who wants two weeks in the sun. The largest resort in the area is Lloret de Mar which has English pubs and clubs, funny hats and rock and is overrun by tourists throughout the summer.

Quieter resorts are also to be found along the Costa Brava and, for those who are prepared to make their own way, there are some delightful, unspoilt villages in this friendly area of Catalonia which preserves a language and heritage distinct from that of the rest of Spain.

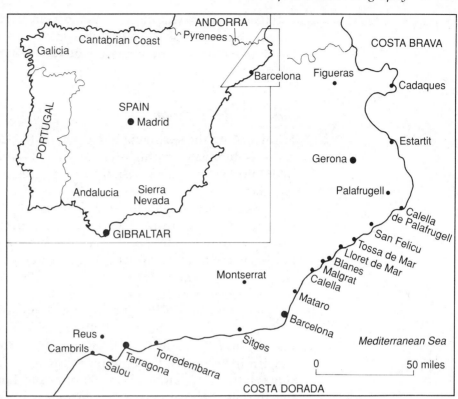

Diagram 5.4 Map of Spain showing the Costa Brava and Costa Dorada

Barcelona

Barcelona, the capital of Catalonia, is a fascinating city in both summer and winter. On the harbour front is the statue of Columbus who set sail for America from Spain. Beside the statue is moored a replica of his ship, the Santa Maria, and further along the quay is the Maritime Museum which has exhibits from all over the world.

Inland from the harbour is the famous Ramblas, a tree-lined street with a central promenade. In Summer, market stalls display their wares and in December the area, both here and outside the medieval cathedral, is a wonderland of Christmas novelties. Wandering through the old Gothic quarter near to the cathedral, visitors can enter coffee shops which take them back through time with their decor and old world charm. At the end of the Ramblas is the fashionable shopping area with El Corte Ingles, a national department-store chain.

Overlooking the city is the hillside of Montjuic where the Olympic stadium has been built and the Spanish Village, or Pueblo Español, has numerous shops and cafes set within its facades, designed to represent the various styles of architecture to be found throughout Spain.

All of this, together with many churches, a bullring, the football stadium and countless museums go to make Barcelona a city of varied and ever-changing interest.

The Costa Dorada

The Costa Dorada, or the 'golden coast', south of Barcelona, has quieter resorts than those to be found to the north. The Costa Dorada is accessible through the airport at Reus.

Sitges has steep winding streets and a long tree-lined promenade, while Salou, which is a little brasher, still maintains a genteel air. The height of its buildings is limited and it has a wide rambla-type promenade stretching for miles.

The Costa Blanca

Further south the skyline of Benidorm on the Costa Blanca, or the 'white coast', is dominated by high-rise apartments and hotels, often reaching to over thirty storeys. The Costa Blanca is accessible through the airport of Alicante.

Benidorm is a resort which might be said to have a split personality. In summer it is the throbbing destination for millions of families and teenagers so that in July or August it is difficult to put a foot between the bodies on the beach. However, in the winter it is a paradise for those who can afford the time to take a break from the winter weather in UK. The beaches are empty and spotless making a beautiful sight with their clusters of palm trees; the weather is calm and warm, rivalling the average British summer; the discos and bars on the seafront resound to the music of tea dances; and the British pensioner reigns supreme in a resort where English is becoming as common as Spanish. Once the summer season returns, the entertainment, restaurants and hotels adapt themselves so that the busiest resort on the Mediterranean can once again offer its clients everything in the way of sand, sea and fun.

Only a few miles out of Benidorm are the villas and apartments of those who prefer to buy their own property and some of these are in fishing ports such as Calpe, whilst others like those in Javea, feature prestigious, landscaped holiday developments.

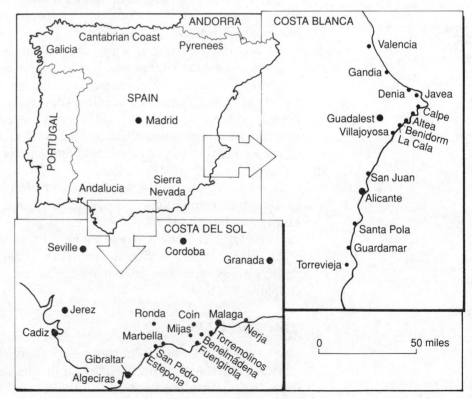

Diagram 5.5 Map of Spain showing the Costa Blanca, the Costa de Almeria and the Costa del Sol

Some brochures offer self-catering accommodation in the villages outside Benidorm but it is worth noting that car hire would be essential if holidaymakers are not to be stranded in these villages.

The Costa de Almeria

The southern coast of Spain has a series of resorts catering for the British market, from the Costa de Almeria to Gibraltar. The Costa de Almeria was opened up, to a great extent, by *Horizon*, who even have a street named after them.

The accommodation on the Costa de Almeria is generally in very modern but Moorish-style hotels and apartments, complete with every amenity. The sun is hot almost every week of the year, as can be testified by the desert-like surroundings in which many a Spaghetti Western was filmed. For those who want guaranteed sun and sand, without being concerned about experiencing Spanish culture, there really could not be a better choice.

The Costa del Sol

Further west is the Costa del Sol, or the 'sun coast', with the traditional resorts of Torremolinos, Fuengirola and Marbella along the coastline of Andalucia. The Costa del Sol is accessed through the airport at Malaga.

Each resort on the Costa del Sol has its own distinct atmosphere with Torremolinos appealing to the younger end of the market and Marbella shedding its up-market image in order to appeal to the average tourist. The more expensive life-style can be experienced at Puerto Banus where the yachts of the wealthy are moored, and it is well worth a visit.

Outside the towns it is quite easy to travel into the hills and encounter the true spirit of Andalucia with its white-washed cottages and brightly coloured flowers. Mijas is such a town which, whilst being commercialised to the extent that it offers a donkey taxi for the tourist as well as numerous gift shops, still retains the charm of a mountain village.

From all of the resorts of southern Spain it is possible to take a trip to Gibraltar. For some it is a nostalgic trip with memories of days in the Services; for others it is simply one more opportunity to buy duty-free goods.

Northern Spain

Whilst these are the main holiday areas for the mass tourist market, Spain has much more to offer. Brittany Ferries will take clients direct from Britain to Spain, landing at Santander.

Although the summer weather is cooler than in the south, the *Cantabrian coast* in the north has beautiful, unspoilt beaches and coves. Further west, the green and beautiful *Galicia* hides behind the mountains revealing its secrets to very few foreign tourists.

To the east are the mountains of the Pyrenees, with the independent principality of Andorra. Trips are arranged to this area from the Costa Brava in the summer, and skiing is becoming very popular in the winter.

Southern Spain

Skiing is also to be found in the Sierra Nevada in the south where it is possible to experience a winter and summer holiday in one during spring when the mountains are cold, but the warm beaches are only a short drive away. The Sierra Nevada mountains also lead to the historical Andalucian cities of Granada, with its Moorish palaces, Córdoba with its fantastic mosque, and Seville and Jerez, the centre of the sherry industry.

Summary for Spain

Capital:
Madrid

Currency:
Peseta (pta). Money can be changed in any bank, most hotels and in the small *bureaux de change* which are located in most resorts.

Getting there:
By air – the main airports are Gerona, Barcelona (del Prat), Reus, Alicante (Altet), Valencia (Manises), Almeria, Malaga, Seville, Madrid (Barajas), Bilbao.

By sea – many British tourists use the route from Plymouth to Santander. Ferries also go to the Balearic Islands from Barcelona, and to north Africa from the ports of Alicante, Almeria, Malaga and Algeciras.

By rail – there are direct trains from Lisbon, Paris and Geneva.

Main interests for British tourists include:
The sun and sand of the 'costas'; the historical attractions of Granada, Cordoba and Seville; the tourist and business interests of Madrid.

Banking hours:
0900–1400 Monday to Friday, 0900–1300 Saturday.

Shopping hours:
Vary, but shops are generally open from 0900 to 2000 Monday to Saturday. They close for a long break in the middle of the day from 1300 to 1600. Larger department stores in the cities may not close in the afternoon.

Special note:
Tourists who take their own cars to Spain are strongly advised to take out a bail bond. This is because, if anyone injures another person in an accident in Spain, they may be jailed while the accident is being investigated. The bail bond means that the person can afford to be bailed out of jail by putting up the necessary money which will be covered by the bond, almost like an insurance.

◊ *Activity 5.2* ◊

1 Spain, as well as other Mediterranean countries, has islands which are very popular with the British tourist. With the aid of an atlas, name each of the islands in the western Mediterranean shown on Diagram 5.6 below.

2 Using brochures and suitable reference material, create a fact sheet for each island containing the following information: nationality; currency; language; capital; airports; ferry connections; main resorts; climate in summer (August); climate in winter (January); traditional or historical attractions; sporting facilities; wildlife interest; types of accommodation; tour operators offering holidays to the island this year.

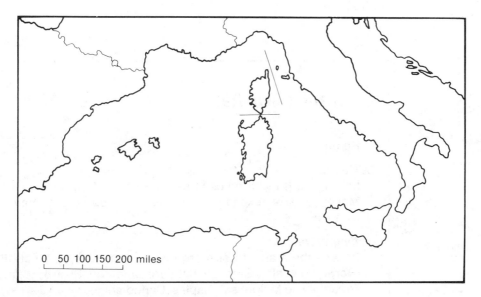

0 50 100 150 200 miles

Diagram 5.6 Western Mediterranean islands

In Activity 5.1 on page 55 you will have coloured in several countries in the eastern Mediterranean. Tourism in Italy is long established and, across the Adriatic, Yugoslavia has consistently developed its tourism since the early 1970s. Greece is a favourite with many British tourists who like the casual, homely approach where they can eat in tavernas, live in studio rooms and really get to know the local population.

Italy

Diagram 5.7 shows the main resort areas in Italy which are popular with British tourists. These can be regarded in three categories, namely:

♦ the Rivieras with their traditional resorts;

♦ the beautiful, tranquil lakes in the north;

♦ Rome and other cities such as Venice, Pisa, Naples and Florence, which have an historical or a business interest.

Italian islands have already been considered in Activity 5.2 on page 67 but further study would reveal the treasures of Italian culture and holidays. Northern Italy offers not only the lakes but skiing in the Alps and fascinating cities such as Turin, Genoa and Milan. Central Italy offers not only Rome with its ancient, modern and religious interest, but also Tuscany with its variety of mountains, countryside and coastline. In Umbria, the 'green heart of Italy' there is the city of Assisi the home of St Francis, as well as many other fine old Etruscan cities. Southern Italy has the city of Naples, overshadowed by Mount Vesuvius and the preserved cities of Pompeii and Herculaneum. Food and drink in Italy is distinctive and many regions have their own special dishes. Wherever a client takes a holiday they will be sure of the traditional Italian friendliness and enthusiasm.

Summary for Italy

Capital:
Rome

Currency:
Italian Lira (L) with notes in denominations from L500 to L100 000. Money can be exchanged in banks, airports and many railway stations.

Getting there:
By air – the main airports are Rome (Leonardo da Vinci), Bologna (Borgo Panigale), Genoa (Cristoforo Colombo, Sestri), Milan (Enrico Forlanini and Malpensa), Naples (Capodichino), Pisa (Galileo Galilei), Turin (Caselle), and Venice (Marco Polo).

By sea – there are ferries to all the main islands as well as some links along the coasts.

By rail – there are main connections from London and Paris.

Main interests for British tourists include:
The coastal resorts, the lakes and mountains, skiing, Venice and other historical cities and sites, and Rome. Vatican City, which holds great attraction for Roman Catholics and others, is a separate state in its own right.

Banking hours:
These vary in different parts of the country, but in general 0830–1330 and 1530–1630 Monday to Friday.

Shopping hours:
From 0830 to 2000 with a long lunch break from 1300 to 1600, except in the north where the break could be shorter. Food shops are often closed on Wednesday afternoons.

Special note:
For tourists who take their own car to Italy there is a scheme to give reduced priced petrol by means of pre-paid petrol coupons. Coupons can be purchased in Britain through the AA or the RAC.

Diagram 5.7 Italy

Yugoslavia

Yugoslavia, while only a hovercraft ride across the Adriatic from Italy is vastly different in culture.

♦ Yugoslavia has five nationalities and three different languages which give rise to a rich culture where the East meets the West.

♦ Tourism in Yugoslavia is state controlled and the standard of accommodation is good and reasonably priced.

♦ The scenery is varied with mountains, lakes, forests, cliffs, bays and a coastline dotted with islands.

In order to see the variety of scenery and culture in Yugoslavia many tourists take a two-centre holiday. These holidays take in a coastal or island resort and a week either in the historical city of Dubrovnik or in the beautiful mountainous hinterland. The National Park of the Plitvice Lakes is particularly beautiful with its chain of sixteen lakes set in forest scenery.

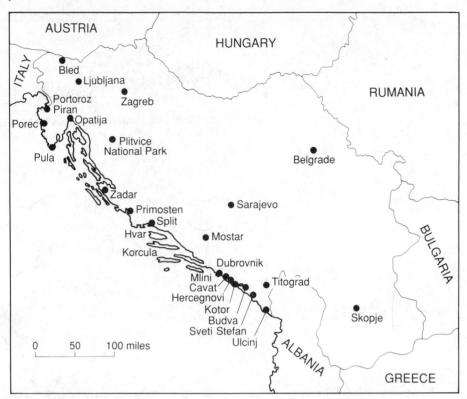

Diagram 5.8 Yugoslavia

Summary for Yugoslavia

Capital:
Belgrade

Currency:
New Yugoslav Dinar (NYD), with one NYD = 100 Para. Travellers cheques and foreign currency can be changed at banks and hotels but receipts should be retained as it is difficult to reconvert dinars into foreign currency.

Getting there:
By air – the main airports are Belgrade (Surcin), Dubrovnik (Cilipi), Ljubljana (Brnik), Zagreb (Pleso), and Split.

By sea – there are ferry connections with Italy and Greece.

By rail – there are express links from London via Paris, Venice and Vienna.

Main interests for British tourists include:
The availability of good holiday resorts, both coastal and inland, at very reasonable prices.

Banking hours:
0730–1200 Monday to Friday.

Shopping hours:
0800–1200 and 1700–2000 Monday to Friday and 0800–1400 on Saturday. Department stores in the major cities stay open all day.

Greece

Greece is the most popular European destination after Spain for package tours. The mainland offers a wealth of culture and history but most UK package holidays are located on one of the many islands. Corfu and Rhodes have enjoyed most popularity over the years.

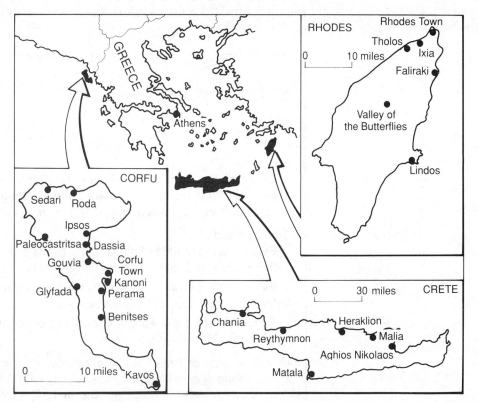

Diagram 5.9 Greece and the Greek Islands

Corfu

Corfu with its lush green countryside is in the Ionian chain of islands just off the west coast of the Greek mainland. In Corfu Town, cricket is still played on the Central Square, recalling memories of British rule from 1815 to 1864. Most resorts are along the eastern coastline with Benitses offering excellent nightlife and Kavos in the south making a complete contrast with a long sandy beach and little in the way of organised entertainment.

Rhodes

Rhodes, in the Dodecanese chain of islands, is just off the coast of Turkey and has a great concentration of holiday accommodation on its northern tip around the main town, also called Rhodes. The presence of a casino probably contributes to the international image which Rhodes has over other Greek islands.

Crete

Crete is the largest and most southerly of the Greek islands and it has its loyal admirers who return year after year. The north of the island has more sophisticated resorts while the south coast has some beautiful, peaceful areas for those who want to get away to tranquility.

The islands of the Cyclades, the Saronic and the Sporades chains have resorts to suit every taste, from the jet-setting Mykonos with its varied nightlife to isolated, sometimes volcanic islands where you can just relax in the sun and the warmth of the local welcome. It is interesting to remember that the Greek word *Xenos* means both stranger and friend.

Summary for Greece

Capital:
Athens

Currency:
Drachma (dr) with one drachma = 100 lepta. Travellers cheques and currency can be changed at banks and exchange counters. Exchange rates can vary between one bank and another.

Getting there:
By air – to the mainland airports of Athens or Thessaloniki or direct to the islands of Crete, Corfu or Rhodes, etc.

By sea – to the main port of Piraeus or on any of the multitude of ferries which connect the islands.

By rail – there is the Athens Express direct connection from London, via Paris, Milan and Belgrade.

Main interests for British tourists include:
The casual way of life to be experienced with Greek hosts who always make their visitors welcome; the historical sites and the variety of scenery and coastline on the many islands.

Banking hours:
0800–1400 Monday to Friday, although banks in some resorts offer currency exchange facilities in the afternoon as well. Banks are closed on Saturday, Sunday and public holidays.

Shopping hours:
These vary a great deal but some shops will be open from 0800 through to 2030. Some take a long lunch break and others, especially corner kiosks may stay open very late.

Alpine Areas

Skiing has become big business in Europe and with the expansion in accommodation it also makes sense to use the resorts in summer as well as winter. Some alpine areas of Switzerland, Austria and Italy have therefore developed a dual role as sports centres, particularly orientated to the young in winter, and walking or relaxation centres for active, but generally older clients in the summer.

◊ *Activity 5.3* ◊

Make a collection of brochures which specialise in skiing or 'lakes and mountains' holidays.

Examine the brochures and then choose two resorts each from Switzerland, Austria and Italy which appear in both kinds of brochures. In this way you will be studying a total of six resorts. For each resort make a chart like the one below and fill in the following information:

	Summer (August)	Winter (February)
Airport used		
Transfer time		
Scenery		
Expected temperature		
Excursions		
Sports facilities		
Shopping facilities		

Accommodation featured in both seasons (using a common hotel and apartment block)
   Price for two weeks full board in the hotel
   Price for two weeks self-catering in the apartment		

Entertainment		

Ski Resorts

Clients who are going skiing may require more specialist attention and knowledge than other package holidaymakers. Some will be experienced skiers who know exactly what they want and where they want to go, but the first-time skiers will need more help.

The availability of snow in a ski resort will depend on the height of the mountain as much as whether or not it is facing the sun from the south. The higher resorts which face north will have snow longer, possibly even into April, but they will also be colder for the first-timer who might be standing around listening to instructions or queueing for lifts. Many villages in Austria are as low as 2000 feet, but the resorts in France which have been specially developed for skiing can be over 6000 feet.

The French resorts offer excellent skiing and accommodation but they usually lack the traditional, fairytale architecture of the older Swiss or Austrian resorts.

If the client is booking a family holiday where not everyone is a skier you will need to consider the surroundings and whether or not there will be enough in the way of sightseeing, shopping and other sports, such as skating or swimming, available for the non-skiing members of the family.

◇ *Revision Questions* ◇

1 Name three countries which are usually featured in brochures as Winter Sun destinations.

2 State the capital of each of the following countries:
a) Switzerland,
b) Denmark,
c) The Netherlands,
d) France,
e) Portugal.

3 Of which countries are the following the capitals?
a) Madrid,
b) Bucharest,
c) Vienna,
d) Stockholm.

4 Name three European countries east of Berlin which feature in brochures for UK tourists.

5 Give one car ferry route operated between the UK and the following countries:
a) France   *From*_____
                  *To*_____
b) Denmark   *From*_____
                  *To*_____
c) Belgium   *From*_____
                  *To*_____
d) Spain   *From*_____
                  *To*_____
b) The Netherlands *From*_____
                  *To*_____.

6 Name three French resorts on the Côte d'Azur.

7 For each of the following areas of Spain, name the gateway airport and one resort which is popular with UK tourists:

a) Costa del Sol,

b) Costa Dorada,

c) Costa Blanca,

d) Costa Brava.

8 Suggest three day-trips which could be made by a businessman who had a few days for relaxation while visiting Madrid.

9 For each of the following name:

a) the largest Spanish island in the Mediterranean;

b) the island whose capital is Valetta;

c) the island where Napoleon was born;

d) the island which has a volcano called Mount Etna;

e) the Greek island group to which Rhodes belongs;

f) the largest Greek island.

10 If you were asked to help some first-time skiers to choose a suitable resort, list three topics you would discuss with them.

6 *Worldwide Travel Geography*

By the end of this chapter you should have increased your:

- ♦ knowledge of travel geography with respect to the USA, Canada, the Far East and Australia;
- ♦ skills in exercising judgement to recommend suitable destinations for clients.

In the previous two chapters we have been able to study some aspects of UK and European travel geography as they affect the British tourist. This chapter will highlight a few areas in the rest of the world which are popular with tourists from Britain.

Holidays for destinations beyond Europe are known in the travel industry as long haul. The most popular long haul destinations for tourists from UK are:

- ♦ the USA,
- ♦ Canada,
- ♦ the Far East,
- ♦ Australia.

The fact that many of the places visited are English-speaking probably stems as much from the fact that the British like to feel comfortable abroad, as from the desire to meet friends and relatives. Many try to combine a stay with friends with a holiday which satisfies the desire to see different scenery or other cultures. So, a holiday to Australia or New Zealand very often includes stopovers in Singapore, Malaysia or Thailand to experience a culture which is totally different from the British in scenery, customs, dress and food.

United States of America

The USA is popular with British holidaymakers for several reasons:

- ♦ many people visit relatives and friends,
- ♦ films and TV shows stimulate interest in the USA,
- ♦ there is a variety of spectacular scenery,
- ♦ English is spoken.

As one holidaymaker commented,

"It is possible to cross the 21 miles between Dover and Calais and feel totally lost in a strange land, yet after crossing three thousand miles to America the British tourist can feel totally at home."

The United States Travel and Tourism Administration (USTTA) have, for the purpose of promoting tourism, divided the States into twelve areas with eighteen **gateway airports**. These areas are as follows:

- The Golden West,
- New England,
- The Great Southwest,
- The Pacific Northwest,
- Southeast Sun Country,
- The Great Lakes Region,

- Eastern Gateway,
- Trails West,
- Southland USA,
- American Pacific Islands,
- Historic Washington Country,
- Western Gateways.

Southeast Sun Country

If you were to ask most people which destination comes to mind when you mention the USA the majority would probably mention Florida as one of their first three choices.

Between 1986 and 1989 the market grew very quickly, rising from only 4 charters per week out of this country to Florida in 1986, to 51 per week only three years later. Since 70 per cent of holidays booked were repeat holidays, this vouches for the fact that the clients had experienced a good quality holiday in a stable, friendly society.

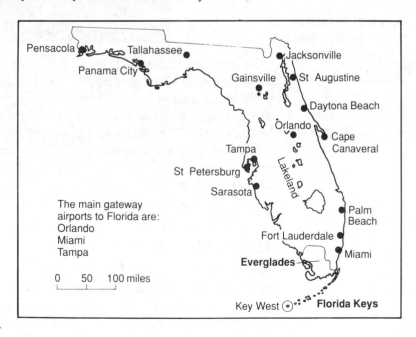

Diagram 6.1 Florida

Orlando in the centre of Florida has the greatest concentration of man-made attractions in the world. Within a hundred mile radius are:

- Walt Disney World
- Seaworld
- Circus World

- Cypress Gardens
- Busch Gardens
- Kennedy Space Centre

Miami is Florida's centre of glamour, romance, excitement, suntans, skyscrapers and nightlife. With high humidity in the summer months, the prices of accommodation drop in April and remain low until mid-December when American tourists arrive for their winter vacations.

Tampa on the Gulf of Mexico is the centre for quieter holidays in charming older resorts with a Spanish flavour. St Petersburg is considered to be the boating capital of America and the Pinellas Suncoast offers 28 miles of sandy beaches and 128 miles of coastline linking eight Gulf Coast resorts. During the summer months there is an abundance of accommodation on this coast both in hotels and self-catering apartments.

*Donald Duck at Walt
Disney World*

Florida is not marketed alone but as part of the Southeast Sun Country which includes North and South Carolina, as well as Georgia and Florida. In the Southeast Sun Country southern hospitality is emphasised as well as the magic of Disney and the wonders of space at Cape Canaveral. Miami's palm-lined shores, along with its glamour and romance are offered as a contrast to the Gulf Coast with its old-world charm and colourful yachting ports. The Carolinas offer a different holiday whether it be golf and hang-gliding attractions, or the scenery of the Great Smokey and Blue Ridge Mountains.

The Golden West

California and Nevada are marketed as the Golden West with the emphasis on sunshine, glamour and adventure.

Los Angeles is a fast-moving city, full of entertainment with the constant excitement of the possibility of seeing a film star. The homes of the stars can be seen in Beverly Hills and memories of old movies can be re-lived on the back sets of Universal Studios.

Disneyland, the original and smaller version of Florida's Walt Disney World, is at Anaheim just outside Los Angeles. Just as in Florida, the Magic Kingdom is divided into Fantasyland, Tomorrowland, Adventureland and Frontierland. Visitors can experience exciting rides and musical parades, and walk down Main Street with Mickey Mouse or Donald Duck.

Diagram 6.2 California

Several hours' drive to the south of Los Angeles is California's oldest city, San Diego which is almost on the Mexican border. Here the visitor can see the old town which has been restored to look like it was 150 years ago, or take part in one of the fantastic shows at Sea World, or go to the beach where surfing is the most popular activity.

A few hours' flight to the north are the steep hilly streets and beautiful bay of San Francisco, a truly cosmopolitan city, both in its people and restaurants. Chinatown has the largest Chinese community of its kind outside Asia, and at Fisherman's Wharf visitors can taste freshly caught crab right out of a steaming cauldron.

Inland is the marvellous Yosemite National Park with some of the highest waterfalls in the world as well as some of the oldest trees dating back to 4000 years ago.

The deserts of Nevada hide the bright lights of Las Vegas, the city that never sleeps. Here is a world of night clubs, casinos and bars with many of

Las Vegas

the top stars and artists performing in some of the best hotels and theatres in the West.

The Grand Canyon is so magnificent that it is difficult to comprehend its beauty and size, and it is probably best viewed from an air tour out of Las Vegas.

New England

On the north-east of the United States is New England, an area which is becoming increasingly popular with British tourists.

New England is already well established as a tourist destination for Americans and Canadians especially in autumn or the Fall as it is called, when the profusion of trees turn a tremendous variety of colours. Although winters can be a bit sharp and cold in New England, summer and spring are very pleasant with only occasional humidity, unlike many other American destinations.

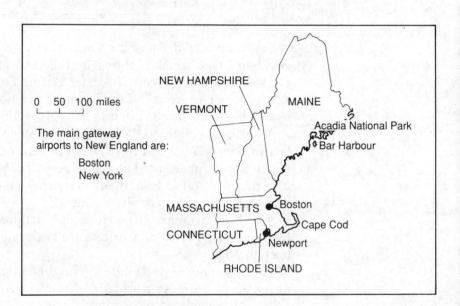

Diagram 6.3 New England

New England has some of the smallest American states, including Connecticut, Massachusetts and Rhode Island, which is not an island at all. The larger states of New Hampshire, Vermont and Maine to the north are beautiful mountainous areas, ablaze with colours in the autumn and a paradise of snow in the winter.

Boston, the capital of Massachusetts, is the cradle of American democracy for it was here that the Boston Tea Party sparked the independent spirit which led to the American Revolution and the Declaration of Independence in 1776. The Freedom Trail is a 3-kilometre walk around the city, marked by red stripes on the pavement, which traces places of historical interest connected with the period of the War of Independence. Boston is regarded as a capital of culture with theatres, museums, parks and two symphony orchestras.

The rest of New England also has many places of interest, including the universities of Harvard and Yale; several living museums depicting life at the turn of the century; and, for the yachting enthusiasts, numerous small ports along the indented coastline.

The Eastern Gateway

Marketed as the Eastern Gateway, New York with its noise, crime and slums still holds a fascination for many people with its variety of entertainment, shopping and commerce, and constant, vibrant bustle and excitement. Manhattan is the original city of New York and here you can visit:

♦ the Rockefeller Center, a complex of twenty-one buildings. These include a business centre, underground shops, the NBC television network centre, restaurants, and an open-air ice rink, or café depending on the season, in the centre of the buildings as well as a fantastic view from the top of the centre.

♦ Fifth Avenue, which once housed the wealthy of the last century and now has exclusive, expensive shops, or stores;

♦ Central Park which offers breathing space and peace in the heart of the city;

♦ Time Square and Broadway, the main area for theatres, cinemas and colourful nightlife.

New York

Historic Washington Country

Washington DC, the capital of the USA, is marketed as Historic Washington Country, and includes the states of West Virginia and Virginia, as well as the federal District of Columbia. Washington DC is a beautiful, southern city with magnificent state buildings, museums and monuments set in green parkland. Many of the main attractions in Washington are freely open to the public. These include:

♦ the White House, the official residence of the President of the United States and home for every President since George Washington;

*The Capitol,
Washington DC*

♦ the Capitol Building which houses the Senate and the House of Representatives;

♦ the Smithsonian Institute which includes the National Air and Space Museum, with some of the earliest aeroplanes right through to the spacecraft Friendship 7;

♦ a magnificent view from the top of the 555-metre high Washington Monument, as well as the peace and tranquility of the nearby Lincoln and Jefferson Memorials;

♦ Arlington National Cemetery where lie thousands of American soldiers who fought from the Revolutionary wars onwards. Here too is the eternal flame to President Kennedy who was assassinated in Dallas, Texas in 1963;

♦ Potomac Park, bordering the river of the same name, which offers many recreational activities.

Summary for the USA

Capital:
Washington DC

Currency:
US Dollar (US$) with one dollar = 100 cents. Money and travellers cheques can be exchanged at banks. American Express travellers cheques can be used virtually as currency, preferably in denominations of $10 and $20.

Getting there:
By air – to any of the 18 gateway airports. The most popular airports for British travellers are New York (JFK International) and Orlando. Visitors to the west coast use the airports of San Francisco or Los Angeles International. Baggage allowance is usually according to the number of pieces of luggage rather than the weight of the cases.

By sea – this is more unusual nowadays, although the *Queen Elizabeth 2* still does a number of trips each year.

Main interests for British tourists include:
Visting friends and relatives; Florida and Walt Disney World; the natural wonders of the National Parks in the west; the attractions of New York in the east.

Climate:
This varies greatly but summers tend to be much hotter than in Europe. Some areas, such as Florida can experience high humidity in summer and other areas, such as the mid-west are extremely cold in winter.

Banking hours:
0900–1500 Monday to Friday.

Shopping hours:
0930–1800 Monday to Saturday, with many supermarkets staying open until later in the evening. Some states permit Sunday trading.

Special note:
1 Visitors should be advised to carry at least one credit card because they are used for identification in the USA and, for example, it is almost impossible to hire a car without a credit card.
2 Cheap coach travel is available for non-nationals but passes should be purchased in the UK from either the Greyhound or the Trailways bus companies.
3 Remember the USA has state as well as federal laws. This means, for example, that laws regarding age limits for alcohol consumption can vary from state to state.

Canada

Canada is a land of such vastness and variety that it is sometimes difficult for Britons to comprehend. Canada covers about 4 million square miles and is the second largest country in the world, after the Soviet Union, yet it has only 23 million people, a mere tenth of the population of the United States and under half the population of the UK. Most Canadians live just north of the border between Canada and the USA, leaving tracts of untouched land to the north whose beauty is largely unspoilt by man and where it is possible to retreat from the busy twentieth century, by fishing and camping in isolation.

Spring is particularly beautiful in Canada with a profusion of blossom trees and, as in New England, autumn, or the Fall, brings a wealth of glorious colours. Winter turns the country into a skiing paradise and summer sees the Canadians take to the outdoor life with zest and enthusiasm.

Western Canada

Western Canada is dominated by the Rocky Mountains, and here National Parks such as Banff and Jasper to the west of Calgary preserve the beauty for visitors to enjoy in comparative comfort. The cities of Vancouver and

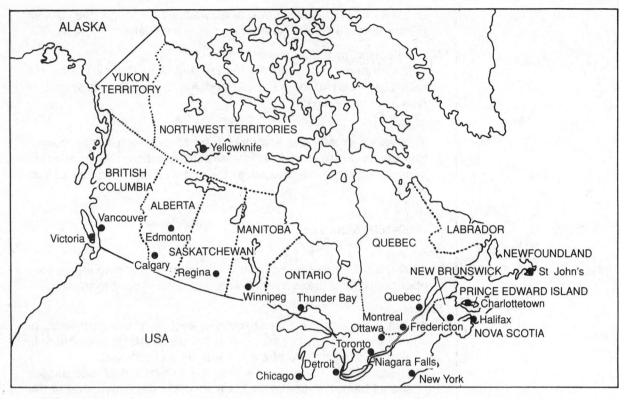

Diagram 6.4 Canada

Victoria offer all amenities but, in contrast, further north the Yukon and
the Northern Territories are the last great frontiers and a haven for
naturalists and those who seek adventure.

Calgary is a great place to experience the thrills of the west, especially at
the famous Calgary Stampede in July when the horsemanship and skills of
the cowboys are tested to their limit in the Chuck Wagon Race. The area
around Calgary also has:

♦ Heritage Park where visitors can ride a steam railroad;

♦ the Dinosaur Park on St George's Island where prehistoric times are
  brought alive;

♦ the ultra-modern sports facilities which were created for the Winter
  Olympics which were held there in 1988.

Eastern Canada

Further east, Toronto and Montreal are great favourites with the British.
Toronto is the provincial capital of Ontario and is the largest Canadian
city. The airport to the north of the city is a major gateway for British
visitors to Canada.

Although Canada is officially bilingual, with equal prominence given to
French and English, the area around Toronto is predominantly English-
speaking. Sights to be seen in and around Toronto include:

♦ the CN Tower which at 1815 feet is one of the world's tallest free-
  standing structures. CN stands for Canadian National, the national
  railway;

- the Ontario Science Centre and the Metro Zoo;

- several unusual recreational and shopping areas such as Ontario Place on the Harbourfront;

- Canada's Wonderland to the northwest and Casa Loma, a fairytale castle to the north of the city;

- a day's trip can be made from Toronto to the Niagara Falls or to the towns of London and Stratford, the centre for the Canadian Shakespearian Festival;

- trips to the more remote regions such as Agawa Canyon in the north can be taken through the rail routes from Sault Ste Marie in the east at the centre of the Great Lakes.

Toronto

Montreal is in the French-speaking state of Quebec, but about a third of the city's population speaks English as their first language. Montreal is the second largest city in Canada and is the business and commercial capital of the country, although the actual capital is Ottawa. There is an unusual series of underground recreation and shopping complexes in Montreal, all linked by a metro system, with every station having a different decor. At the highest point of the city is the Mont Royal Park affording a haven of peace and tranquility in a modern, bustling city.

The provincial capital is Quebec, the only walled city in North America, and it has a true French atmosphere with sidewalk cafés, religious shrines, carriage rides and a culture dating back to the French occupation of the area in the early seventeenth century.

The great St Lawrence River flows right through the region and at its mouth are some beautiful sights on the Gaspe Peninsular and at Percé Rock.

Summary for Canada

Capital:
Ottawa

Currency:
Canadian Dollar ($) with one dollar = 100 cents. As in USA a five cent piece is also called a nickel, the 10 cent piece is called a dime and the 25 cent piece is called a quarter. Travellers cheques are best brought in Canadian dollars which are widely negotiable.

Getting there:
By air – the airports most frequently used by British tourists are Toronto, Montreal, Calgary and Vancouver.

By sea – Montreal is the only port for passenger liners from Europe.

By rail – there are several connections with USA including New York to Montreal, Chicago to Toronto and Detroit to Ottawa.

Main interests for British tourists include:
Visiting friends and relatives, sightseeing at Niagara Falls and visiting the National Parks in the west.

Climate:
Varies in such a large country but generally the summers, from May to September are warm, and the winters are very cold with snow. British Colombia in the west is the mildest state with very warm summers and relatively mild winters.

Banking hours:
1000–1500 Monday to Friday.

Shopping hours:
0900–1800 Monday to Friday with late night shopping until 2100 Thursday and Friday. Some shops also open on Saturday.

Special note:
1 Canada has two official languages – English and French. The French-speaking areas are in the east of the country, mainly in the state of Quebec.
2 Smoking has been banned in most public areas in Canada.

◇ *Activity 6.1* ◇

While on work placements use the brochures and reference material available to you to compose a letter in answer to the one below.

```
                                          32 Wood Crescent
                                          Halsall
Travelworld                               Lancashire
High Street
Downholland
Lancashire

Dear Sir/Madam,
          Thank you for arranging the tickets for us to
attend my cousin's wedding in Chicago. It is wonderful news
that we will be able to take up to three free flights in North
America. We are quite pleased really that we have to return
to Chicago for our flight home to Manchester because we will
have a chance to say goodbye to the family – goodness knows
when we shall be over again! My husband and I are really
looking forward to the trip but with so much to see and only
three weeks to do it we would appreciate your advice.
     I would like to see some of the fantastic scenery we have
heard about and my husband would really like to play on a good
golf course. Please write with some suggestions as to which
flights we should book and maybe then we can make up our
minds.
     Thank you for your assistance,

          Yours sincerely,
          Pat O'Connor
```

The Far East

As flying becomes both faster and cheaper, long haul destinations are becoming more popular. Diagram 6.5 indicates some areas of the Far East, including Singapore, Hong Kong and Thailand which are popular with British tourists *en route* to Australia and New Zealand, and also more and more as holiday destinations in themselves. For each of the countries on the map you should find out the names of the capital cities and the gateway airports.

Singapore

The Republic of Singapore, a former British colony, is an island at the tip of the Malaysian Peninsula, to which it is joined by the Johore Causeway. Singapore is one of the busiest ports in the world and has

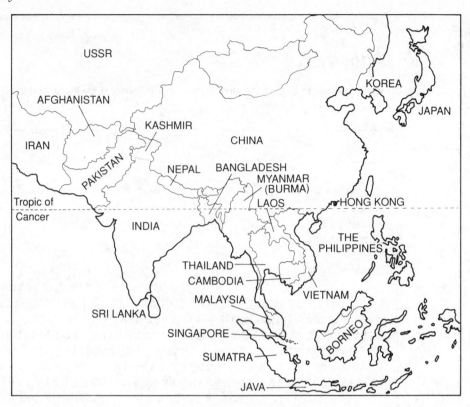

Diagram 6.5 Countries of the Far East

a vibrant, international atmosphere which is hard to resist. The climate in Singapore varies very little throughout the year, being almost always hot and humid, although the monsoon rains from November to January can bring frequent, heavy downpours.

Singapore has many attractions for the tourist including:

♦ the Van Kleef Aquarium,

♦ the Jurong Science Centre and Bird Park,

♦ the famous Raffles Hotel,

♦ Sentosa Island in the harbour, which has been developed as a modern tourist complex.

It is said by many that it is hard to decide whether Singapore or Paris offers the best restaurants in the world, but certainly Singapore cannot be outdone in its variety of both eastern and western food.

Hong Kong

Hong Kong, which is currently a British territory, will be handed back to the Chinese nation on 30 June, 1997. It is mainly a business centre and has the highest density of population of any place on Earth. With a land area of only 400 square miles, Hong Kong has a population of over five million giving a density of 12 500 people to every square mile. Compare this with a density of 600 per square mile in the UK, 260 per square mile in France and only 8 per square mile in the USA.

The climate in Hong Kong is hot and humid in summer, and cool and sunny in winter. Probably the best time of the year to visit Hong Kong is in the autumn when the temperature and the humidity drop and days are clear and sunny.

There are some attractive islands and countryside to visit around Hong Kong, but most people go for the shopping, entertainment, nightlife and restaurants. Most shopping in Hong Kong is duty-free and the area around Cat Street is noted for very cheap oriental antiques, while the Stanley area is excellent for clothes. The Tiger Balm Gardens appeal to visitors of all ages and the Sung Dynasty Village re-creates a Chinese village of a thousand years ago.

Thailand

Thailand with its capital Bangkok epitomises all the mysteries of the East. Bangkok has over 300 temples, each one a fine example of Thai art and tradition. However for all its tradition, the city still vibrates to discos, nightlife and what are euphemistically called massage parlours.

Outside of the city are some beautiful resorts, including:

♦ Chiang Mai to the north;

♦ the seaside resort of Pattaya, two hours drive from Bangkok, set on the Gulf of Siam and offering an abundance of watersports;

♦ Phuket which is an hour's flight from Bangkok and lies on the Andaman Sea, a backwater of the Indian Ocean with some of the best beaches in Thailand.

Bangkok is a shopper's paradise and bargaining is a must in most places, although the better stores tend to have fixed prices. Good buys include Thai silks, cotton, precious stones, silver, bronze and pottery antiques.

◇ *Activity 6.2* ◇

Make a special study of one Far East destination of your choice.

Imagine you work for a travel promotion company called New Looks and your particular speciality is taking slides to assemble a ready made package on a given area. Select twenty locations you would wish to photograph in your chosen Far East destination. Give your twenty slides appropriate titles and write a brief commentary for the tape to be used with them.

Australia

With the present trend for Australian programmes on our television channels, many Australians could possibly feel quite at home here, but British tourists going there find a totally new and different world. Australia is as large as the USA or the whole of Europe. From Sidney in the east to Perth in the west it is over 2 500 miles, and from Adelaide in the south you have to travel over 2000 miles to Darwin in the north.

The Australian climate varies from tropical, humid and wet in the north to hot, dry desert in the centre, and milder weather in the south, with

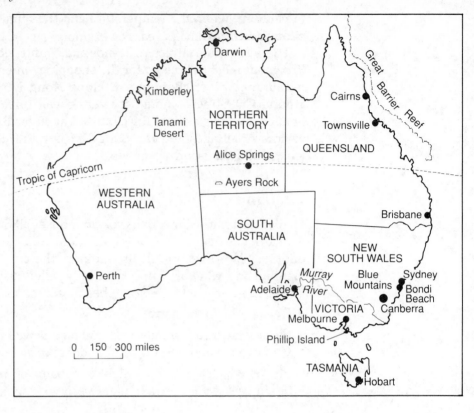

Diagram 6.6 Australia

skiing becoming popular along the border between the States of Victoria and New South Wales.

Many British tourists go to Australia either to experience a true adventure holiday in the outback or to visit friends and relatives, often on the east or south coast.

Adventure holidays, camping or using small hotels can be taken by coach, rail or genuine 'jeep'-type vehicles. Such holidays can be booked with several reputable specialist tour operators and can last from 16 to 40 days. The areas usually covered by adventure holidays include Kimberley in the north-west with its spectacular scenery filled with gorges and enormous chasms, and the Tanami Desert with traces of old mining towns and even dinosaur tracks.

In the southern part of the Tanami Desert are the Macdonnell Ranges with the old telegraph station of Alice Springs. This remote town in the dry red centre of Australia is an ever more popular tourist destination and can even boast a casino. About half a day's drive away is the haunting Ayers Rock with its Aboriginal caves and paintings. The rock rises straight out of the desert and changes to fantastic colours especially in the sunset. It is easy to understand why it is a place of special significance for the Aboriginal population.

Other adventurous holidays are offered in the east of the country centred on the coral islands of the Great Barrier Reef and the crocodile farms further north.

Most British emigrants to Australia settled around the cities of Sydney, Melbourne and Adelaide and each of these has places of interest in the surrounding area for the British visitor.

From Sydney it is possible to experience the variety of Australia in a comparatively small area. For example:

♦ inland are the Blue Mountains, so called because of the fine blue mists given off by the many eucalyptus trees;

♦ even further inland the adventurous can experience the utter emptiness of the outback;

♦ on the coast, there are many beautiful beaches, including the famous Bondi Beach;

♦ to the north frequent flights will take the visitor to Brisbane or the coral beauty of the Barrier Reef in Queensland.

Sydney itself with its unusual Opera House in the harbour, can offer all the amenities one would expect in any big city and the capital, Canberra, is only a short flight away.

Melbourne, one of the oldest Australian cities has interesting architecture which blends the new with the old. In the surrounding area these are:

♦ the Dandenong Range of mountains;

♦ Gippsland, a lush, fertile area dotted with unspoilt lakes and forests;

♦ Philip Island Nature Reserve, south of the city which is home to koalas and fairy penguins as well as other wildlife only to be found in Australia.

Adelaide in South Australia has a very attractive coastline with excellent white sandy beaches. Adelaide has a very European atmosphere, probably due to the large number of German settlers in the area. German settlers in the 1830s started the wine centre in the Barossa Valley where tourists can take tours through the small villages with their Lutheran churches and German restaurants.

Another favourite with tourists in the Adelaide area is a trip along the Murray River on a genuine steamboat, recalling images of the Mississippi in the United States of America.

Summary for Australia

Capital:
   Canberra

Currency:
   Australian Dollar (AU$) with one dollar = 100 cents.

Getting there:
   By air – to Sydney, Adelaide, Melbourne, Perth, Brisbane and Darwin. There is a departure tax levied on all international departures. Within Australia there is a wide network of internal flights.

   By sea – international cruise lines dock at Sydney, Melbourne, Hobart, Fremantle, Adelaide and Brisbane.

Main interests for British tourists include:
   Visiting friends and relatives, and adventure holidays.

Climate:

This varies from semi-tropical in the south to very dry desert in the centre and hot tropical weather in the north. The summer time in Australia is in December and January.

Banking hours:

In general these are 0930–1600 Monday to Thursday and 0930–1700 Friday, although there is variation from these times in some parts of the country.

Shopping hours:

Large stores are open 0900–1730 Monday to Friday and 0900–1200 Saturday. Late night shopping is until 2100 on Fridays in Melbourne, Adelaide, Brisbane, Hobart and Darwin. Late night shopping is until 2100 on Thursdays in Sydney, Canberra and Perth. Smaller shops tend to stay open until late every night.

Special note:

All visitors to Australia need to obtain a visa.

◇ *Revision Questions* ◇

1 Name the country in which you would find each of the following: Yosemite; Phuket; Sentosa; Ayers Rock; Fisherman's Wharf; Milford Track; Pattaya; Bondi Beach; Barossa Valley; Sea World.

2 State the capitals of each of the following countries: Australia; Thailand; China; India; Japan.

3 Suggest three excursions which could be made by a business traveller who had a few days for relaxation while visiting Bangkok.

4 Of which countries are the following capitals? Kathmandu, Kuala Lumpur, Rangoon, Manila, Jakarta.

5 For each of the following name:
a) A wine producing area in Australia;
b) A country famous for its silk garments;
c) The area in the Far East which has the highest density population;
d) A tax-free shopping paradise in the East;
e) A small island in the Far East which is an independent republic;

f) The largest island in the world;
g) A gambling city built in the middle of a desert;
h) The smallest American State;
i) A walled city in North America.

6 In which city or town would you find the following:
a) The Freedom Trail;
b) Tiger Balm Gardens;
c) Raffles Hotel;
d) A Canadian Cowboy Festival held in July;
e) The Rockefeller Center.

7 In connection with North America, what do you understand by 'the Fall'?

8 Suggest three excursions which a family with a 10-year-old child might take while on holiday in Singapore.

9 On the borders of which countries are Niagara Falls to be found?

10 Name the capital of Canada.

7 *Tour Operations*

By the end of this chapter you should have increased your:

♦ **knowledge of the different types of tour operators, the basic elements of a package holiday and types of reservation systems;**

♦ **skills in observing and recalling information about different tour operators with regard to their reservation systems, late booking systems, variety of brochures and associated companies.**

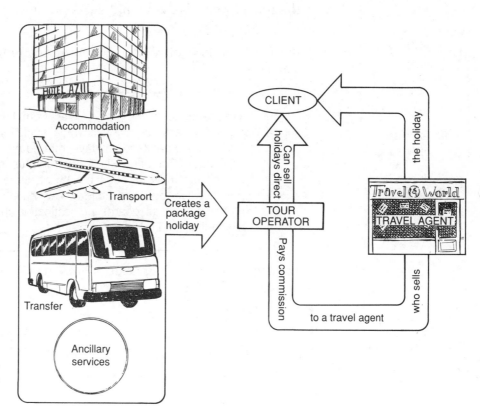

Diagram 7.1 Tour operators and travel agents

Before we look in detail at the components of a package holiday, examine the brochures on the shelves of any travel agent and do Activity 7.1 on page 94 which builds on the brochure study you started in Activity 5.1 on page 55.

◇ *Activity 7.1* ◇

1 Refer to the map you coloured in for Activity 5.1 on page 55. The yellow colour indicates summer destinations, the red colour indicates winter destinations. Try to draw a line on your map dividing the countries featured in the summer brochures only, from those which appear in both summer and winter brochures.

2 In Activity 5.1 on page 55 you also looked at skiing and city break brochures. Now, make a list of at least ten other different types of holiday brochure.

3 You will have noticed that some tour operators produce more than one type of brochure. Make a list of brochure titles produced by at least one tour operating company. Which two tour operators produce the greatest number of brochures?

4 Keep the brochures you have collected so that you can refer to them as we study different types of tour operators and package holidays.

Travel agents stock brochures to sell package holidays on behalf of tour operators, from whom they receive commission. In the next three chapters we shall consider:

♦ the role of tour operators in the travel industry today;

♦ the costing of brochures;

♦ the legal position of tour operators if anything goes wrong with a holiday.

> The name tour operator derives from the alternative name for package holidays which is 'inclusive tours' or ITs. The first package holidays, offered by such people as Thomas Cook and Sir Henry Lunn, usually involved touring around European places of interest. However nowadays a package holiday can have a variety of meanings both as regards the destination and the way in which the holiday is taken.

Whatever the form of a package holiday, it will be offered in a brochure with a fixed price for:

♦ accommodation;

♦ transport;

♦ **ground arrangements**, such as transport from the airport;

♦ other ancillary services, such as car hire.

Types of Tour Operators

There are three main types of tour operator:

♦ **inbound** tour operators,

♦ **outbound** tour operators,

♦ **domestic** tour operators.

Inbound Tour Operators

Inbound tour operators provide holidays, tours and tourism services for visitors coming into their country. We already saw in Chapter Three that some inbound tour operators in the UK have joined together to form BITOA. However the brochures of these members of BITOA would not have been among those you examined in a travel agency during Activity 7.1 on page 94 because travel agents in the UK are concerned with selling holidays to British people, not holidays for foreigners coming into the country.

In Activity 7.1 on page 94 you may however have come across some brochures which specialised in a particular country. Some of these brochures are produced by state controlled organisations and are concerned solely with inbound operations to their country.

Outbound Tour Operators

Outbound tour operators produce package holidays for UK residents wishing to holiday abroad. Holidays abroad can be taken to:

♦ **short haul**,

♦ **medium haul** or

♦ **long haul** international destinations.

Diagram 7.2 gives an indication of the countries within each of these areas.

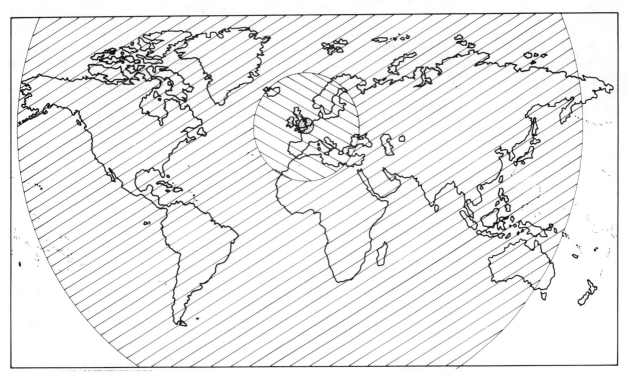

Diagram 7.2 The world showing travel zones

　　Short Haul　　　　Medium haul　　　　Long haul

- ◆ Short haul destinations are those closest to home, such as northern France, Belgium, Holland and parts of Germany and Scandinavia. These destinations are ideal for short breaks, very often centred on the main cities, for three or four days.

- ◆ Medium haul destinations are in the sunny areas of Europe with which many people associate the package holiday. These areas include Spain, the South of France, Italy, Yugoslavia, Greece and North Africa. On average, flights to such destinations take from two to four hours and holidays will be taken for at least a week, but more generally for a fortnight. These journeys are sometimes classified as short haul destinations.

- ◆ Destinations further afield to countries such as the USA, Canada, Australia and the Far East are regarded as long haul. Flights can take from 8 to more than 30 hours and generally holidays will be taken for at least two weeks and very often for longer periods.

	Hours of flying time	Possible destinations	Usual length of stay
Short haul	1–3 hrs	Paris Belgium Holland	Few days to a week
Medium haul	2–4 hrs	Spain French Riviera Greece	1–2 weeks
Long haul	8–30+ hrs	USA Canada Far East	3–6 weeks

The table above summarises information with regard to international destinations, the flying time involved, and usual length of holidays taken.

Domestic Tour Operators

Not all brochures stocked by travel agents offer holidays abroad. Tour operators who offer holidays in this country are called **domestic** operators and flights between British airports are called domestic flights. The term domestic applies to the whole of the UK so it would apply to holidays in Northern Ireland, the Isle of Man or the Isle of Wight as well as mainland Britain. Domestic holidays are regaining popularity lately, particularly for weekend breaks and second holidays.

Types of Package Holidays

Many package holidays are to a single destination where the client stays in the same accommodation for the full week, fortnight or however long the holiday lasts. The most common single destination holidays are offered in the summer and winter brochures which are produced by all the large tour operators. Single-centre holiday brochures may be produced with a particular group in mind, such as young people under 30, or older people over 55. The destinations, hotels and entertainment offered in the brochures are all planned with the particular age group in mind. Brochures may cater for special interests as varied as golf or painting. There is a wide range of brochures offering all kinds of activity or sporting holidays. The largest group of these are the skiing holidays.

Some tour operators offer touring holidays for a client to see all the sights of an area. Tours of the Far East can involve a client spending three or four nights in each of several different countries. For example it is possible within a three week holiday to visit Singapore, India and Thailand.

Cruising is a special form of touring with the possibility of three months sailing right around the world or, if you do not have the time, you can be flown out to join the ship for a specific part of the cruise. Cunard offer fly/cruise holidays to the Caribbean where it is possible to fly by Concorde from London and then cruise around the islands for a week or two before flying home.

Some tour operators package holidays which include the flight from the UK, hire of a camper or car and vouchers for hotel accommodation to be used as and when the client wishes. Such touring holidays are particularly popular in the USA and Australia and are referred to as **fly/drive** holidays.

Multi-centre holidays are where the client stays in two or more hotels or other accommodation, usually in contrasting areas. Two-centre holidays are popular in Yugoslavia where the client can, for example, spend one week in Dubrovnik and then a second week on a quiet off shore island.

The Main Components of a Package Holiday

Accommodation

The variety of accommodation offered in package holidays is enormous to cater for a full range of taste and the circumstances of the client. It is the role of the travel agent to point out the distinctions between types of accommodation and to assist the client to make a suitable choice. At the time of booking the client's main concern will probably be the resort or the flight time, but, once they have arrived in the resort, the hotel facilities, including the type of bedroom will assume new importance.

The client's first choice is between accommodation in a:

♦ hotel, with a bedroom and some meals included in the price, or

♦ self-catering with rooms but no meals included in the price

Hotel meal arrangements can vary between:

♦ bed and breakfast basis, sometimes called **Continental Plan** (CP);

♦ Half board, sometimes called **Modified American Plan** (MAP);

♦ Full board, sometimes called **American Plan** (AP).

Half board in this country usually means bed, breakfast and the evening meal but abroad it is becoming more and more common for it to mean bed, breakfast and either the midday or evening meal. The travel agent will need to check this out with the tour operator.

Full board means that all three meals are provided and, if the client wishes to go out for a full day, a packed lunch can be ordered. Packed lunches vary greatly from hotel to hotel with the larger hotel chains providing excellent boxed picnics including soft drinks.

In many brochures the client has the choice of half board or paying a daily supplement for full board.

Hotels in the USA and the Far East do not normally include any meals in the basic price, although a restaurant is usually provided on site. This board arrangement is known as **European Plan** (EP).

Hotel rooms can be:

♦ single rooms,

♦ twin rooms with two single beds,

♦ double rooms with a double bed and

♦ family rooms which may be described as three-bedded, four-bedded, or simply large rooms.

Single rooms can be very small without facilities such as a balcony or they may be larger rooms which would normally take two or more people. In the UK, single rooms are usually smaller than average, but in European resorts where the hotel's rooms may be all of a standard size, a supplement may be charged for the sole use of a larger room.

A double room is almost always available in British hotels but is more unusual in hotels in the rest of Europe.

The standard of family rooms varies from hotel to hotel but the tour operator will have details on whether the rooms are genuinely large or if the hotel management will simply put a roll-up bed on the floor.

Hotel rooms in American hotels normally have two large double beds as standard, sleeping up to four people. As the price will be for the room this type of accommodation is very economical for a family, but not so much for a couple or a single person.

Extra facilities can be booked at some hotels. Such facilities might be:

♦ a balcony,

♦ a sea view from the room,

♦ a room on the ground or the top floor,

♦ a room over the swimming pool.

Sometimes a supplement has to be paid for these extra facilities. Some booking forms provide boxes to be ticked for the facilities required.

Meal requirements

If the hotel offers a choice of meal requirements, please tick the correct box.

Full board	FB	
Half board	HB	
Bed and breakfast	BB	
Room only	RO	

Room facilities

If you have confirmed private bath shower toilet or balcony, please tick here.

Bath or shower	B	
Toilet	T	
Balcony	BA	

Diagram 7.3 An extract from a booking form

If such facilities are described as being 'available in most rooms' but no boxes are provided to be ticked, then the client's requirements should be noted in the special requests box on the booking form.

Special requirements

If you have any special requirements, such as a ground-floor room, a cot or special meals, please indicate these in the space below.

Diagram 7.4· The special requirements section from a booking form

Apart from hotels, accommodation may be provided in pensions or guest houses giving clients the opportunity to mix with local people. This type of accommodation is offered by some tour operators using tavernas in Greece or small guest houses in Malta.

Self-catering could be offered in:

♦ studios,   ♦ tents,
♦ apartments,   ♦ caravans,
♦ villas,   ♦ boats.

All self-catering accommodation includes:

♦ cooking facilities   ♦ living space
♦ use of a bathroom   ♦ sleeping areas

A studio is usually a room containing the bed, sitting area and a small kitchenette. Apartments have at least one separate bedroom as well as a sitting and kitchen area. Villas can vary in size and sometimes come with their own private swimming pool.

Camping in tents, caravans or even barges is becoming very popular both in this country and abroad. Some tour operators specialise in camping holidays where the tents are already put up on site and all necessary equipment is provided. Flotilla holidays are available where clients can book a yacht which joins a group sailing in a specific area with a guide. Flotilla holidays are very popular in the waters off Yugoslavia and Turkey.

ACCOMMODATION

	Bedroom	Kitchen and living area	Breakfast	Breakfast plus one meal	Breakfast plus two meals	Alternative description
Self catering						
Studio		√				
Apartment	√	√				
Villa	√	√				
Tent	√	√				
Caravan	√	√				
Boat	√	√				
Hotels						
Room only	√					European Plan (EP)
Bed and breakfast	√		√			Continental Plan (CP)
Half board	√			√		Modified American Plan (MAP)
Full board	√				√	American Plan (AP)
Guest houses/tavernas	√		√	possibly		

Diagram 7.5 Summary chart of types of accommodation

The overall standard of the accommodation for both hotels and self-catering is usually indicated by a star or other rating. In the UK there are nationally recognised standards such as:

♦ AA stars,
♦ English Tourist Board crowns,
♦ Channel Island suns.

Countries such as Spain have their national system of classification, but in addition some tour operators list their own ratings. This may be a system of lettering associated with the name of the company, so Thomsons have a T rating system which works in a similar way to the AA star rating – the higher the number of Ts, the better the hotel standard.

Rating systems are only provided as a guide to clients and it is sometimes worthwhile comparing the descriptions of an apartment or hotel abroad in more than one brochure. Travel agents can also refer to the agents' *Hotel Gazetteer* which provides a frank 'warts and all' description of accommodation offered in the tour operators' brochures.

Transport

Package holidays can be offered with travel by:

♦ coach   ♦ ship

♦ rail   ♦ air

There is an increasing tendency for some tour operators to offer a choice in their brochures for clients to travel by either air, rail, ship or coach to the same resorts and accommodation. Some tour operators offer arrangements for travel whereby a client can book a personalised holiday with all the advantages of a package holiday but more flexible times and dates for travelling.

Coach transportation can be offered from a local pick up point right to the resort. The facilities on board the coach will include:

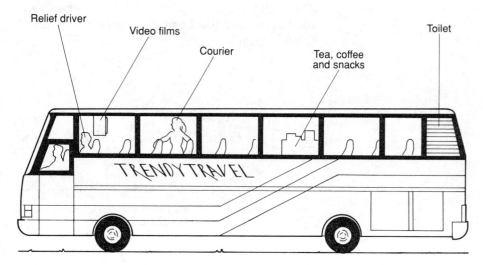

Diagram 7.6 Coach travel

Rail travel can also be provided from a local station and extra facilities can be booked, such as:

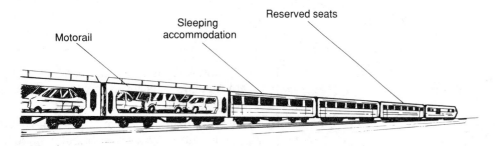

Diagram 7.7 Rail travel

Travel by sea may be:
♦ on a cruise
♦ or simply the ferry crossing to France, Belgium or Holland.

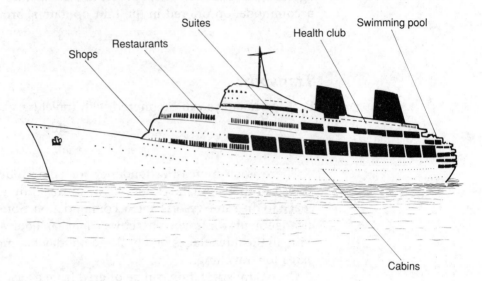

Shops Restaurants Suites Health club Swimming pool Cabins

Diagram 7.8 Liner travel

About 85 per cent of holidaymakers still prefer to travel to their destination by air, in spite of delays at airports and tight security measures. Tour operators use both charter and scheduled flights in their package holiday arrangements.

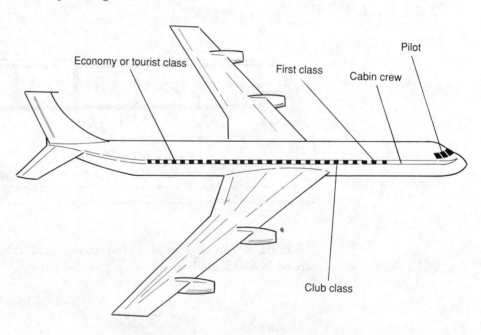

Economy or tourist class First class Cabin crew Pilot Club class

Diagram 7.9 Air travel

> ♦ A **charter flight** is commissioned for a specific period of time and usually flies a full load of passengers to a given destination.
> ♦ A **scheduled service** operates to a timetable and is committed to fly whether or not the aircraft is filled.

To offset the fixed costs of flying on scheduled routes, the airlines offer special group inclusive tour rates (**SGITS**) to the tour operators. Package holidays which make use of seats on scheduled aircraft are referred to as **Inclusive Tours by Excursion** or **ITX**.

Aircraft may be chartered for a specific flight or over a period of time, such as for six or twelve months. This type of charter is known as a **time charter**. More commonly in the package holiday trade an aircraft will be chartered for a **flight series** making it available for example at the same time each week for specific flights.

By using flight series charters, tour operators can reduce costs and aim to fill their aircraft to a destination. They can book clients who are going to different resorts and hotels which are in the same locality, on the same aircraft. This type of operation is known as **back to back** because the flight out is filled with holidaymakers and the return flight will bring others home.

One disadvantage of flight series charters is that inevitably there will be an empty flight home at the beginning of the season and an empty flight out at the end of the season. These empty flights are referred to as **empty legs**.

Sometimes, if bookings are poor from a specific airport a tour operator will require clients to take a flight from another airport. This way of changing flight arrangements is known as **consolidating**.

Package holidays which make use of **chartered aircraft** are referred to as **Inclusive Tours by Charter** or **ITC**.

◊ *Activity 7.2* ◊

Some tour operators have their own aircraft while others always charter from a specific airline. Use your study of brochures, as well as your time on work experience to add to the following list of tour operators and their associated airlines.

Tour operator	Airline
Thomson Holidays	Britannia Airlines
Enterprise	Air 2000

Ground arrangements

A person travelling independently must find their own way from the airport to the hotel, but on a package holiday the tour operator will have made these arrangements in advance. These are called ground arrangements. Package holidays bring foreign travel within the budget of many people. However many of these people are travelling for the first time and the support given by the tour operators in their ground arrangements can be very important.

For work abroad looking after the ground arrangements, tour operators recruit and train **couriers** to:

♦ provide the hotels with rooming lists from information received from the UK office;

♦ meet clients on arrival in the resort;

♦ show clients to their accommodation;

♦ help clients to enjoy their holiday;

♦ assist with general enquiries, usually providing a file of information about the local area, banks, doctors, shops, pubs and excursions;

♦ sort out any potential problems;

♦ look after children;

♦ provide entertainment in the evenings, especially on long stay holidays for retired people;

♦ make arrangements for clients who are ill to see a doctor;

♦ make arrangements for clients who need repatriation;

♦ escort clients to the departure point at the end of their holiday;

♦ help clients who have serious problems to fill out a company report giving details of the complaint.

Diagram 7.10 shows a typical rooming list with names of clients, number of nights they are staying and their required room type, including any special requests.

Couriers or overseas representatives are sometimes recruited by the UK office, usually with some knowledge of a foreign language. On the other hand they may be foreign nationals, or Britons married to local nationals, recruited by the overseas office.

Transfers or the transport to the booked accommodation may be in the form of a waiting taxi, but more usually nowadays it will be by coach. The larger tour operators can have a dozen or more coaches meeting a specific flight so first-time holidaymakers should be advised to check their transport carefully. Clients travelling by coach to their destination normally have a courier as well as a driver on board for the whole of the journey.

Couriers are usually available throughout a package holiday. In the larger hotels there will be a team of couriers so that at least one is available throughout the day. Smaller hotels and apartments may receive a daily visit but in some more remote areas there may simply be a telephone number for contacting the courier.

For each resort area, a tour operator will have an office and Area Representative. This local office will:

♦ supervise the couriers,

♦ check flight details,

♦ make transfer arrangements,

♦ maintain contact with the hoteliers and apartment managers,

♦ maintain contact with the UK office and

♦ organise excursions to local attractions.

Normally these offices are not open to the public because the clients' point of contact should be the courier for their hotel or apartment.

```
┌─────────────────────────────────────────────────────────────┐
│                         ABC TOURS                            │
├─────────────────────────────────────────────────────────────┤
│                       Rooming List                           │
├─────────────────────────────────────────────────────────────┤
```

For hotel: AMARAGUA	**Updated on:** 14 August
Arrival date: 25 AUGUST	
Flight number: AO 123	
From MAN	**To** PMI

Room type	Facilities	No. of nights	Passenger names	Requests
TR	PB, WC, SV	7	MR. W. ARMSTRONG MRS. M. ARMSTRONG MS. S. ARMSTRONG	COT
TW	PS, WC, BC	14	MR. E. WALSH MRS. P. WALSH	—
TR+B	PB, WC	7	MR. T. O'CONNOR MRS. P. O'CONNOR MST. D. O'CONNOR MISS. A. O'CONNOR	LOWEST POSSIBLE FLOOR
SI	PS, WC, SV	7	MS. A. HORNER	—

SI = Single	PB = Private bath
TW = Twin	PS = Private shower
TR = Triple	WC = Toilet
+B = extra bed	BAL = Balcony
	SV = Sea view

Diagram 7.10   A tour operator's rooming list

Ancillary Services

On some holidays extra facilities or services can be provided at extra cost. These services include:

- car hire,
- excursions,
- hire of skis and boots,
- ski school.

Look at some skiing brochures and you will see that apart from the accommodation and transport, they also offer the hire of skis and ski boots as well as a few hours of tuition each day. It is worth remembering that such extras on a skiing holiday can be expensive and the client should be made aware of the total costs involved.

Car hire is available as an extra in most brochures. The cost varies from country to country, as well as according to the length of hire. Car hire for a week is usually at a cheaper rate than hire for a few days. Some tour operators have been known to offer ridiculous car hire rates such as a pound for the first week but the client should be helped to read the details of costs for any subsequent weeks. Most car hire does not include Personal Accident Insurance or **Collision Damage Waiver** so the details should be checked and the client made aware of the total cost of the extra insurance.

Excursions, which can be pre-booked, are normally arranged by the courier with a local coach company and for the first-time traveller are good value for money. Not only will the client be taken to the local places of interest but a courier will accompany the group to give help and information. The commission from these excursions usually plays a significant part in the earnings of the couriers.

Functions in Tour Operating

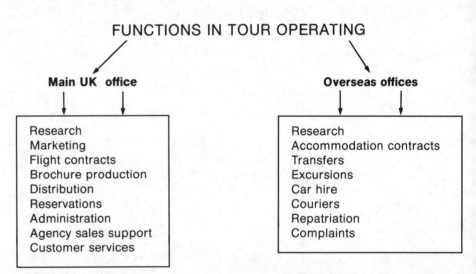

Diagram 7.11

Diagram 7.11 summarises the main functions in tour operating, some of which have already been mentioned. In the next chapter we will look at brochure production, including accommodation and flight contracts. Research, marketing and distribution will be considered in Chapter Eleven.

Agency sales support

Agency sales are promoted by UK representatives who are employed by the tour operators to visit travel agencies. UK representatives have the task of ensuring that travel agents receive sufficient publicity material and brochures and that these are prominently displayed. Some representatives arrive unannounced in an agency to observe the image being portrayed for their company.

The larger operators sometimes cooperate with travel agencies in promotions at local travel fairs or with Travel Trades Clubs in sponsorship of entertainment. At these events the UK representatives have an opportunity to promote the latest brochure product. On average it is agreed that it takes eight to ten brochures to produce one firm booking. About 80 per cent of the bookings for the larger operators is done by only 20 per cent of ABTA travel agents.

In 1971 Cosmos were the first to restrict distribution of brochures but now it is common practice. Travel agents can argue that they cannot make bookings if they do not have brochures, but most tour operators will now only send brochures in proportion to the past bookings.

Administration

The administration section:

♦ produces invoices,

♦ receives payment,

♦ despatches tickets.

Diagram 7.12 shows the key timings involved in the booking of a package holiday.

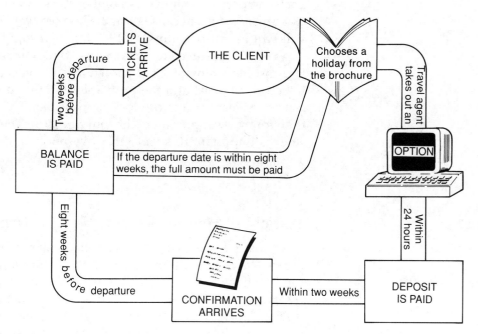

Diagram 7.12 Key timings during the booking of a package holiday

Customer Services Department

The customer services department deals with customer enquiries and complaints. In responding to complaints, the customer services department will always refer to the brochure in their initial dealings with a client. The role of this department is one of conciliation since they are expected to placate a disappointed client and come to some agreement whether it be an apology or some compensation, without having to resort to outside intervention.

Sometimes an *ex gratia* **payment** is offered to a client. This payment is made on the understanding that the tour operator is not accepting any liability or responsibility for whatever has gone wrong with the holiday. The payment is simply made as a goodwill gesture on their part.

A litigation section within the customers services department will be responsible for dealing with any serious complaints which actually come to court. Chapter Nine gives more details about action which could be taken by ABTA or the courts.

Reservations

Reservations departments can have systems, which are either manual or computerised. All reservations systems work on the idea that there is a stock of holidays and an up-to-date count of what has not been sold is always available. Package holidays involve reservations for:

- flight seats,
- hotel beds,
- apartments,
- berths,
- car spaces on ferries,
- tent sites on camp sites.

Each component is shown as a unit of stock. A twin room will be shown as two units of stock because it can be booked by two people, each of whom will require further units of stock for their flight seat or berth.

As bookings are made, so the units of stock are subtracted from the total and the remaining stock is shown as still available. Pricing on package holidays is crucial and the profitability of the tour operator depends on selling as many units of stock as possible. The up-to-date situation is therefore very important to the tour operator. The current state of units of stock is important to ensure that overbooking does not occur.

Wallchart Manual Reservation Systems

The most popular manual reservations system is that which uses wallcharts. Wallcharts are produced at the beginning of the season showing the available units of stock for flights, beds, berths and any other reservable units. On each chart there are marks or flags to indicate each unit of stock. When the travel agent telephones the tour operator a reservation clerk checks the charts and, if the required holiday is available and the booking is **confirmed**, the reservation clerk crosses off the mark or removes the flag from the wallcharts. For a booking of two airline seats and a twin room, four flags would be removed from a wallchart.

The main advantages of a manual system are:

- that the large wallcharts can easily give an overall picture of the current booking situation and for this reason they are still used by some companies as a backup to other systems;
- that they are cheaper than a computerised system for a small independent tour operator.

The main disadvantages of manual systems are that:

♦ they are time-consuming to produce;

♦ their accuracy depends on several users all keeping the information up-to-date.

Card Manual Reservation Systems

The card manual reservation system is similar to using wallcharts but instead of just showing a mark or flag, a card is produced for each unit of stock. When a holiday is booked the cards are removed from their trays and placed in an envelope. In this system a room in a hotel would have one card showing whether it was a twin, three-bedded or larger room. If a holiday was booked for a family of three flying to a resort and staying in a three-bedded room, three cards would be removed for the flight seats and one for the room making a total of four cards. These would be placed in an envelope to be passed to the administration section.

The card system makes more efficient use of the time of the reservation clerk as the trays of cards can be placed near to the telephones. However it does not give the overall picture of the current booking situation that is achieved by the wallcharts.

Computerised Reservation Systems

Computerised reservation systems can be accessed through a reservation clerk by telephone, or offered by the tour operator for direct access by the travel agent via a Viewdata system. Computerised systems have to be interactive so that units of stock can be removed by only one user at a time. This is achieved by the computer programmer who will also build prompts and safety checks into the system. Once holidays are confirmed, units of stock are removed and placed on other computerised files of information which are used for invoicing, payments and ticketing. The basic ideas of a computerised system are similar to the manual systems but the transactions can be made much more quickly.

The advantages of computerised reservations systems are listed below:

♦ The travel agent has more information readily available so that the client can be helped to make alternative choices if their preferred holiday cannot be booked.

♦ In the systems which are available to travel agents, the tour operator no longer has to employ as many reservation clerks.

♦ The system of taking out **options**, whereby a holiday is temporarily reserved for a client until the end of the following day, is more efficient on a computerised system.

♦ Electronic payment is possible, whereby the tour operator can debit the travel agent's bank account directly at the end of each month.

♦ The introduction of Viewdata systems has made it easier for tour operators to make cheaper last minute holidays available and to keep these constantly updated.

◇ *Activity 7.3* ◇

1 Copy out the table below and make use of visits to travel agents to add to the list.

Tour operator	Reservation system	Late booking system
Thomson Holidays	TOPS	Square Deals

2 Some reservations systems are accessed through networks such as ISTEL. Make a list of systems on at least three such networks.

Sources of Income

There are several main sources of income for a tour operator.

♦ Holidays bought from the summer brochure can account for 55 per cent of the company's turnover for the larger tour operators.

♦ Winter and specialist programmes earn about 15 per cent of the tour operators' income.

♦ Interest is earned on money held. **Deposits** can be paid by clients up to eight or nine months before departure and the balance will be paid eight weeks before departure. This money accumulates for the tour operator who receives interest on it.

♦ Commission on insurance, car hire, flight-only sales and excursions is paid to the tour operator. Most tour operators offer their own insurance in the brochure and commission on this can be as high as 37 per cent. Car hire attracts a large commission of up to 25 per cent.

♦ Charges are made for any cancellations or amendments made to bookings. These charges are to cover administration costs but, especially in the case of cancellation charges, there is always a chance that they will recoup the money anyway if they resell the holiday.

♦ Foreign currency is a source of income if the tour operator speculates well and buys currency when the rate is favourable, to use later in the year.

♦ For tour operators who have their own airlines, duty-free goods can be a lucrative source of extra income.

Current Affairs in Tour Operation

Changes in tour operating are reported in the travel press such as the *Travel Trade Gazette* (TTG). As this is a fast-moving industry there are quite often changes in companies involving takeovers and mergers. These changes may be between companies offering competitive products resulting in an increased range being made available to the client.

Alternatively the changes may mean the takeover by a tour operator of a company in another sector of the trade, so extending their influence in the market.

These mergers or takeovers can give the company more scope and lead eventually to better pricing for the client. By keeping abreast of the news in travel, and discussing topics when you are on work placement, you should be able to build up a picture of large organisations such as Thomson Holidays which owns several companies in different sectors of the travel trade.

◇ ***Revision Questions*** ◇

1 Describe two advantages that a manual reservation system might have over a computerised system.

2 Name three major components of a package holiday.

3 What name is given to the practice of tour operators hiring aircraft?

4 List five different types of holiday brochures.

5 Flights which take more than eight hours from the UK to their destination are known as _____ haul.

6 What do you understand by Modified American Plan or MAP?

7 Name four items for which a client may be asked to pay a supplement.

8 What is the word used to describe the practice of asking clients to change their flight, if aircraft cannot be filled for a certain time or airport?

9 Describe four ways in which a courier in a resort could help your clients.

10 Apart from profit on package holidays, list four alternative sources of income which are available to tour operators.

8 *Costing of Brochures*

By the end of this chapter you should have increased your:

♦ knowledge of basic brochure costings, taking into account fixed and variable costs, pricing strategies and the use of mark-up;

♦ skills in calculating commission, from the point of view of both the tour operator and the travel agent, and mark-up.

The brochure is the client's means of knowing the holiday which is being offered. It is also the basis of the legal **contract** between the tour operator and the client and it is therefore important for the information in the brochure to be accurate and comprehensive.

The brochure should have:

♦ information about the resort, accommodation, transport, price, departure dates;

♦ a booking form;

♦ booking conditions showing clearly the responsibilities of both the tour operator and the client;

♦ details of any extra services such as insurance or car hire.

The production of the brochure depends on the size of the tour operator. Most ABTA tour operators are small specialist operators and their brochure may be only a leaflet for a specific tour or a small booklet covering a season's holidays. The larger mass tour operators produce a number of brochures during the year. All produce a summer and winter brochure and most nowadays have a few specialist products such as Lakes and Mountains, or Skiing.

Brochure costings depend very much on the number of brochures produced and with the large operators the print run can be more than a million copies. Diagram 8.1 (page 113) gives a very rough guide to an outline timetable for production of a brochure.

Contracting

In order to be able to offer holidays with certainty the tour operator must contract the flights or other means of travel, accommodation, services such as transfers and car hire rates. In negotiating contracts, the tour operator is concerned both to establish the availability of these elements and to obtain

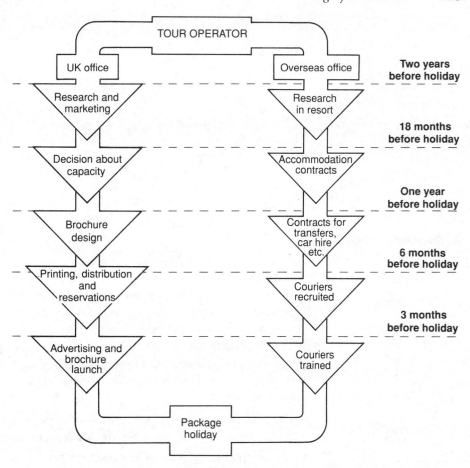

Diagram 8.1 Outline timetable

a realistic price which allows the holidays to be offered to the public at an attractive price and at the same time be profitable for the company.

Contracts drawn up with airlines detail:

♦ the flights to be used,

♦ the costs involved and

♦ any penalties to be paid on either side if the contract is not fulfilled.

Scheduled airlines usually agree to an **allocation** of seats, which means the number of seats made available to the tour operator. A date will be agreed, after which the airline is at liberty to sell those seats to others if the tour operator has not taken the full quota. This date is referred to as the **release date**. With charter airlines it is usual for the tour operator to pay a deposit of 10 per cent initially and then the balance after each flight.

Aircraft can only make money when they are flying. In fact, on the ground they are incurring airport expenses, so the tour operator and airline will aim to make the maximum use of each flight. Sometimes the same aircraft can be used to make flights from more than one airport.

If, for instance, the airline flies from Manchester but does not have an aircraft based at Birmingham, the tour operator may arrange for clients to be taken from Manchester to Malaga, return from Malaga to Birmingham, take clients from Birmingham to Malaga and finally return with passengers for Manchester. This type of flight pattern is known as a 'W' flight plan as can be seen from Diagram 8.2 (page 114).

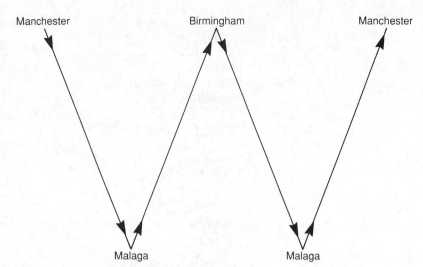

Manchester   Birmingham   Manchester

Malaga   Malaga

Diagram 8.2 The 'W'
flight plan

In order to keep the aircraft in the air as much as possible it is usual for there to be at least three flights per day in summer and two flights per day in winter for each chartered aircraft.

The contracts for accommodation are drawn up after negotiations by UK and overseas staff in the larger companies, or with the help of an agent abroad in the smaller companies. The accommodation contracts can be of three different forms.

♦ The tour operator may be committed to paying for an agreed number of beds, regardless of whether or not he can actually fill them.

♦ A more popular way of contracting accommodation is by **allocation**, where a number of beds are available to the tour operator until the release date, which can be four to six weeks before the holiday date.

♦ The third way of contracting accommodation is on an ***ad hoc* basis** where the tour operator requests accommodation by telex as and when the client requires it.

	Advantages	**Disadvantages**
Tour operator committed to paying for an agreed number of beds	Tour operator can demand a good price	Any unsold beds will add to the tour operator's overall costs
Allocation of a number of beds until an agreed release date	A reasonable price can be negotiated and the tour operator reduces the risk involved	After the release date, the tour operator will have to telex the hotel about availability
Contract accommodation on an *ad hoc* basis	No risk involved for the tour operator	More expensive for the client

Diagram 8.3 Types of
contracts for
accommodation

Diagram 8.3 summarises the main advantages and disadvantages of each of these ways of contracting. Whichever method is used the contract will include:

- details of the types of rooms available, whether they be single, twin, three or four bedded;
- the meal arrangements, including special diets;
- the reservation and porterage procedures;
- any special facilities, such as those for the disabled;
- fire and safety precautions;
- acceptable health conditions in areas such as the kitchen;
- personal accommodation for a courier, and space for a desk and notice-board.

Holiday code	ABC 235	
Resort	TORREMOLINOS	
Hotel	VILLA DE MAR	
Meal arrangement	HALF BOARD	
Departure airport	BIRMINGHAM	
Departure day	SATURDAY	
Departure time	13.30	
First departure	4 November	
Last departure	21 April	14 April
Number of nights	7	14
Departures between		
1 Nov–19 Nov		
20 Nov–3 Dec		
4 Dec–14 Dec		
15 Dec–20 Dec		
21 Dec–29 Dec		
30 Dec–25 Jan		
26 Jan–21 Feb		
22 Feb–31 Mar		
1 Apr–15 Apr		
16 Apr–24 Apr		

*Diagram 8.4
Accommodation and
price grid*

Once these contracts are drawn up, the pricing, as described below, is done and the price tables are sent to the printers. Diagram 8.4 (page 115) shows the kind of information which will be required for the printing of price tables. The Holiday Code is used to identify the package holiday in the reservation system. Other details required include:

♦ the resort,

♦ hotel or accommodation,

♦ meal arrangements,

♦ departure airport,

♦ the actual day and time of flying,

♦ the length of the season.

Down the left hand side the price grid outlines the departure periods for pricing. In Diagram 8.4 all departures which fall between 1 and 19 November will have the same price and then the price will increase or decrease in the next band, according to the price strategy adopted by the company.

Pricing strategy in larger tour operating companies will be considered after you have done Activity 8.1.

◇ *Activity 8.1* ◇

Collect five summer and five winter brochures and examine the price tables for holidays in Spain. Copy the grid below and fill in the details.

Summer brochures	Dates: from	to		Winter brochures	Dates: from	to
Cheapest prices				Cheapest prices		
Most expensive prices				Most expensive prices		
Other dates				Other dates		

We shall return to this activity when considering the pricing of holidays but for now we should note that:

♦ the most expensive dates are called the **high or peak season**;

♦ the cheapest dates are called the **low season**;

♦ the other dates are referred to as the **shoulder season**.

Basic Costings

We have already seen that the tour operator must pay for transport, accommodation and transfers. In addition brochure costings will take the following into account.

♦ The **fixed costs** of the tour operator which include staff salaries; rent; heating, lighting and cleaning for both UK and overseas offices; advertising and brochure production, chartered transport.

♦ The **variable costs** of holidays which include tickets on scheduled services and inflight refreshments. These costs vary with the number of passengers because they only have to be paid for the people who actually travel.

♦ The commission paid to travel agents.

♦ Profit.

The smaller specialist tour operators, who make up most of the ABTA membership, usually cost the basic elements of the holiday and then add a **mark-up** of 20 to 35 per cent to cover fixed costs, travel agent's commission and profit. The larger tour operators are more conscious of the prices of their competitors and introduce a pricing strategy. This could mean that holidays in the low season are offered at the **break even point** where no actual profit is made, but holidays in the peak season are inflated to cover fixed costs, agent's commission and profit.

Selling without profit is regarded as better than not selling at all, especially if the tour operator actually owns airlines and hotels. However, as we saw in Chapter Two the collapse of Court Line and Clarksons, the biggest tour operator of its day, have shown that reducing prices to a bare minimum can be a risky business.

Most package holiday calculations involve the idea of a **load factor**. This means the percentage of the airline or hotel which is actually used. A chartered flight has to be paid for whether the aircraft is filled or not. Operators could make their costings, for example, on the assumption that the plane would be at least 90 per cent filled. This 90 per cent is the load factor. Some charters hope to achieve an even higher load factor, whereas scheduled airlines often work to a load factor as low as 55 or 60 per cent.

Assume that a tour operator contracts a flight series for a 130-seater Boeing 737 every Thursday at a cost of £12 000 per return flight. The season covers 28 weeks and there is an empty leg at the beginning and at the end of the season. This gives a total of 29 return flights:

29 flights at £12 000 = £348 000

The actual cost of a flight with passengers is:

£348 000 divided by 28 = £12 429 per flight

The aircraft holds 130 passengers but a **load factor** of 90 per cent would assume only 90 per cent of 130, that is 117 passengers, would actually fly. Therefore 117 passengers are expected to cover the cost of the flight. The cost per person will be:

£12 429 divided by 117 = £106.23

If more than 117 people book, then the extra fares are clear profit for the company. If less than 117 book, then a no profit, and even a deficit, situation will occur. In this case a decision may be made to consolidate flights and ask clients to fly at another time or from another airport.

Now we will consider how the different tour operators might approach a reasonable costing for the brochure.

The transport cost per person for the flight was	£106.23
Assume the hotel cost per person per week is	70.00
Transfers come to	7.00
Cost per person would be	£183.23

This £183.23 is required to cover the client's actual costs and now the operator must calculate a price at which fixed costs and travel agent's commission can also be covered. About 3 per cent will also be built in for profit. This final price is referred to as the **break even point**.

There are two main ways of calculating the final selling price. The smaller operators often add a mark-up to cover these costs, so:

Cost per person	£183.23
Mark-up of 20 per cent	36.65
Total	£219.88

The small tour operator could then round up £219.88 to a selling price of £220.00 which would be charged throughout the season.

Larger tour operators usually cover the cost of travel agent's commission and then adjust the price according to the season. Refer back to Diagram 8.4 to see the ten different price bands used throughout the season. Most travel agents receive 10 per cent commission from the tour operators, but those who do more bookings than average will receive a bonus, or **over-rider** commission which could be 2 or 3 per cent above this.

If the travel agent is to receive 10 per cent of the final selling price this means that the tour operator must add another one ninth to the cost arrived at above, so:

Cost per person	£183.23
Plus $\frac{1}{9}$ for travel agents' commission	20.35
Selling price of	£203.58

Just check this figure back again if you are not convinced about the one ninth. Ten per cent of £203.58 is £20.35.

The tour operator could now round up this £203.58 to a selling price of £204.00. The pricing strategy might then be to:

♦ sell the holiday at this price of £204.00 in the **low** season, knowing that immediate costs would be covered;

♦ the price could then be raised to £250.00, for example, in the **peak** season and

♦ £222.00 in the shoulder season.

The clients who travel in the **high** and **shoulder** seasons are in effect paying for the fixed costs and profits for the whole year.

This is a very simple example but it should serve to show the reasoning that could go into producing a price grid which varies throughout the season. The actual calculations for the brochure studied in Activity 8.1 on page 116 would be far more complicated but our purpose at present is simply to understand the reason for a price strategy.

Look again at the prices you listed in Activity 8.1 on page 116 from the winter brochures. You will see that the cheapest prices include some dates in December, but the dates of holidays which will include Christmas and New Year come into the peak season. The operator knows there will be enough people looking for holidays at Christmas time to be able to increase the prices without fear of losing custom.

◇ **Activity 8.2** ◇

Look at the travel agent's commission from two points of view. Copy the tables below and fill in the missing spaces.

1 The travel agent receives 10 per cent commission:

Holiday price (£)	Commission earned (£)	Amount due to tour operator (£)
652.00	65.20	586.80
724.00		651.60
1593.00	159.30	
395.00		355.50
2410.00	241.00	

2 The tour operator pays 10 per cent commission:

Net revenue required (£)	Agent's commission (£)	Holiday price (nearest £)
139.23	15.47	154.70 (155.00)
254.17	28.24	
192.00		213.33 (214.00)
372.91	41.43	
504.00		560.00

Sometimes a travel agency acts rather like a tour operator when they prepare **Independent Inclusive Tours (IIT)**. To prepare these they use commission rates from principals in transport and hotels. Like the small tour operator, such a travel agent would add a mark-up to cover fixed costs and some profit. This is becoming more and more common now that agents have direct access via Viewdata to principals' booking systems. The following Activity will help you to calculate an IIT and will also serve as a revision of the principles involved in calculating a brochure price.

◇ *Activity 8.3* ◇

You are asked to cost a holiday for an English couple who wish to spend four nights in Barcelona. You can get 9 per cent commission on the air fare of £175.00 and 8 per cent commission on the hotel price of 7000 pesetas per night for a double room. They would also like a car for five days and you can get 15 per cent commission on the regular price of 8000 pesetas per day.

If the exchange rate is £1.00 = 209 pesetas and your company requires a mark-up of 20 per cent, what would you charge your clients? The following outline can be copied and used as a guide for your calculations.

AIR FARE
£175.00 less 9 per cent	=	£	
2 airfares at	=	£	

HOTEL
7000 ptas less 8 per cent	=		ptas
4 nights at	=		ptas
divided by 209 (ROE)	=	£	

CAR
8000 ptas less 15 per cent	=		ptas
5 days at	=		ptas
divided by 209 (ROE)	=	£	

Total	£	
Total plus 20 per cent mark-up	=	£
You will charge your clients	£	

◇ *Revision Questions* ◇

1 Describe the three ways in which a tour operator could contract accommodation for package holidays.

2 In connection with an allocation of scheduled airline seats, what do you understand by a release date?

3 A tour operator's programme may be divided into three seasons: a) Peak, b) _____, and c) _____.

4 With regard to the costing of package holidays, what do you understand by break even point?

5 On an aircraft, what is the term used to describe the number of seats sold as a percentage of the number of seats available?

6 Briefly describe two ways in which a tour operator might price the holidays in a brochure to cover all costs, commission and profit.

7 List four essential items which should be included in a brochure.

8 If a tour operator is drawing up a contract with a hotel, list four elements which should be included.

9 What do you understand by the term 'variable costs' in connection with brochure pricing?

10 Why are load factors important in brochure costing?

9 Tour Operations and the Law

By the end of this chapter you should have increased your:

♦ knowledge of types of contracts, the law of torts and damages, travel case-histories, relevant Acts of Parliament and the ABTA Conciliation and Arbitration schemes;

♦ skills in critically reading Booking Conditions and advising clients about possible lines of procedures when problems arise.

Contracts

In Chapter One we saw that the role of the travel agent is that of intermediary between the tour operator and the client. The travel agent acts on behalf of the tour operator, who is called the principal. The travel agent also acts as the agent of the client who can expect professional advice and information from the agent. Once the booking has been confirmed and the deposit paid, there then exists a contract in law between the client and the tour operator.

If problems occur with a package holiday it is very important for the travel agent, who may be the first person contacted by the client, to be aware of possible consequences. Problems may be the fault of:

♦ the tour operator,

♦ the hotelier,

♦ the airline,

♦ the travel agent,

♦ or the client.

This chapter will give some background knowledge about who might be in the wrong and what action the client could be advised to take.

A client who books a package holiday enters into a legal contract with the tour operator who should provide the holiday as presented in the brochure. A contract is an agreement which can be either written, oral or, implied.

A written contract is the one we are used to in travel where the details are written down and the contract is signed. The written contract comes in the booking form and its details are outlined in the booking conditions.

An oral contract is one which is spoken and agreed between the parties. This can happen where a client phones for a late booking, pays by credit card and arranges to pick up the ticket at the airport. The client has not signed any contract but nevertheless the ticket ought to be waiting at the airport.

An implied contract is where the client has every right to assume that certain items or conditions are included in an agreement. For example, if a client books a hotel room the presence of a proper bed and bed linen in the room is implied.

Booking Conditions

Look at the booking conditions in any well-known holiday brochure. It may be called Booking Conditions, but it may also have a name such as Fair Trading Charter or Agreement or Policy. Whatever the title, the booking conditions should not be printed on the reverse of the booking form which will be retained by the travel agent once it has been signed by the client.

Booking conditions are divided into two sections.

♦ One deals with the client's contract with the tour operator.

♦ The other deals with the responsibilities of the tour operator to the client.

In most booking conditions, the client agrees:

♦ to pay a deposit,

♦ to pay the balance within a specified time and

♦ to pay an amendment fee if any alterations are requested.

Cancellation charges are also detailed and these usually range from the deposit only, if the cancellation is made early enough, to the full cost of the holiday if it is cancelled on or after the departure date. The booking conditions also normally give advice as to how the client can make known any complaint if the holiday goes wrong.

If you cancel your holiday

The amount payable depends on when we receive your written instructions – the more notice you give, the less we will charge.

Period before departure within which we receive your written cancellation.	Cancellation charge as a percentage of the cost of the holiday, excluding insurance premium.
More than 42 days 29–42 days 15–28 days 1–14 days Departure date or after	Deposit only 30% or deposit if greater 45% or deposit if greater 60% 100%

Diagram 9.1 Table of cancellation charges

The tour operator's section of the booking conditions usually promises:

♦ to supply the holiday as in the brochure;

♦ possibly a guarantee on price;

♦ a list of circumstances under which the tour operator would be entitled to make changes, and a statement as to whether or not these should be regarded as major changes.

According to the ABTA Code of Conduct for tour operators, clients are entitled to receive compensation for major changes such as, if:

♦ the resort is changed to a lower category of accommodation than that booked,

♦ the flight time is changed significantly or

♦ the client is asked to travel from, or return to, an airport which is inconvenient.

If the changes made by the tour operator are so drastic that the client is asked:

♦ to go to a resort in a different country from that booked, or

♦ to accept a flight which is changed by more than twenty-four hours,

then the Code of Conduct states that the client can regard this as a cancelled holiday and claim a full refund.

> For any major alterations the booking conditions specify a scale of compensation fees which could be paid to the client. In the brochure of a registered ABTA member, details will also be given of the special complaints procedure available through ABTA.

If we change your holiday

Period before departure within which a major change is notified to you or your travel agent.	Compensation per person.
More than 56 days	Nil
43–56 days	£10
29–42 days	£20
15–28 days	£30
0–14 days	£40

Where changes are beyond the control of the tour operator, as in the case of a hurricane, an earthquake, the threat of war, riot, civil strife, industrial dispute, terrorist activity, nuclear disaster, or fire, the tour operator is not required to comply with these compensation scales. Such circumstances are sometimes referred to as Acts of God or **force majeure**.

◇ *Activity 9.1* ◇

Using the booking conditions from a well-known tour operator's brochure answer the following questions:

1 How many weeks before the date of departure must the balance of the holiday be paid?

2 What is the normal charge made by the company if your clients wish to change any detail of the booking?

3 When can your clients expect to receive the final invoice for their holiday?

4 Give two examples of major changes which the company might make to your client's holiday and for which the client would receive compensation.

5 Apart from compensation, do your clients have any other alternative if the holiday is changed?

6 If a major change is notified six weeks before the departure date, how much compensation will the company pay to each of your clients?

7 In what circumstances would your clients not be entitled to such compensation?

8 How long is a client given to lodge a complaint about a holiday with the company?

9 If a client cancelled a holiday five weeks before the departure date what percentage of the cost of the holiday would be payable to the company?

10 How should your clients inform you if they wish to cancel their holiday?

The Law and Booking Conditions

The statements made in the Booking Conditions are covered by a number of laws.

The Unfair Contract Terms Act, 1977 forbids the tour operator to try to say that they are not responsible for any problems which might arise on a holiday. For example, tour operators cannot write into the booking conditions that they are not responsible for what happens on a holiday because they do not own the hotels. Whether or not they own the hotels, tour operators are still responsible for seeing that the hotels meet acceptable standards, as described in the brochure.

The Fair Trading Act, 1973 forbids any unfair or unreasonable terms or conditions being imposed on the clients. For example, tour operators cannot say in their booking conditions that all complaints have to be reported within twenty-four hours of returning from the holiday. This would be unreasonable because the client may have suffered injuries or distress which meant they were not in a position to complain immediately.

When signing the booking form a client is, in effect, agreeing to the booking conditions and entering into a **contract** with the tour operator. As the agent of both the tour operator and the client, the travel agent should be sure that the client understands these conditions and is over eighteen, and therefore an adult in law able to enter into the agreement.

Travel law, as indeed any other branch of law in this country is based not only on legislation, or Acts of Parliament such as those mentioned above, but also on case history.

Case Histories

> Case histories are judgements which have been made in the past by a judge in a court and the decisions made have implications for other cases which can be shown to be similar.

Before considering other Acts of Parliament we shall look at some case histories connected with travel and holidays.

> The first story is that of Mr Jarvis (Jarvis v. Swan Tours Limited [1973]) who booked a 15-day skiing holiday in Morlialp, Switzerland from the 1969/70 brochure. The brochure promised a 'house party' atmosphere, with a special resident, English-speaking host and excellent skiing conditions. In fact there were only 13 people in the hotel during the first week and he was entirely alone for the second week! The hotel owner could not speak English and the entertainment was provided by a local man in his working clothes singing a few quick songs one night. The food was very poor and the bar only opened one night – hardly a 'house party' atmosphere! Add to all this the fact that there was no representative available in the second week and the ski runs were far away from the hotel and Mr Jarvis' disappointment and frustration were understandable.

The trial judge decided that the tone and wording of the brochure were misleading and he awarded Mr Jarvis damages of half the cost of his holiday for breach of contract.

> However, the story did not finish there, because Mr Jarvis appealed and the appeal judge then decided that he had not only been a victim of breach of contract but had also suffered mental stress as a result of the holiday. The appeal judge awarded Mr Jarvis twice the original cost of the holiday, considering the mental stress caused by his disappointment and vexation.

Sometimes a case is brought to court by the Crown prosecutor rather than by an individual. These cases can be recognised by the use of 'R' for Regina or Queen in their title, and they are criminal rather than civil cases. The difference between these types of offences will be explained in more detail later.

> In the same year of 1973 another case, (R. v. Sunair Holidays Limited [1973]) was heard. In this case the brochure had stated that a swimming pool was being constructed for the following season. When the client arrived at the resort the pool was almost ready but could not be filled.

The trial judge found that the tour operator was guilty. On appeal the second judge decided that the brochure did not actually say that the pool would be ready, but only that it was being constructed for that season. The appeal judge decided that the tour operator could not be held liable for statements made about an event in the future.

> In 1974 Thomson Holidays were brought to court because the amenities in a Greek hotel did not match up to the standard described in the brochure (R. v. Thomson Holidays [1974]). The interesting point about this case is that in fact two cases were heard. Thomson Holidays pleaded guilty to the first case and then on the second case they tried to claim that they could not be convicted a second time for the same offence.

The judge ruled that in fact an offence was committed every single time a client read the incorrect information in the brochure, so long as no steps were taken to correct it.

About ten years later, in 1984, in the case of Wings Limited v. Ellis, a Mr Wade had booked a holiday from the Wings Faraway Holidays Winter brochure. His holiday was to be in an air conditioned hotel in Nogombo, Sri Lanka, and a photograph of the hotel was shown in the brochure. As it transpired the photograph was of the wrong hotel and in fact there was no air conditioning.

The magistrate found Wings Limited guilty, but the tour operator took the case to the appeal court. The appeal judge then decided that in fact they were not guilty of recklessness because they had informed travel agents and clients of the mistake as soon as they found it. Unfortunately, in this particular instance, the system had broken down and Mr Wade had not received the corrected information in time. This was regrettable, but not a criminal offence. So long as the tour operator sets up a system to inform travel agents and clients of a mistake they have done all that can be expected in the circumstances.

Trades Description Act, 1968

This Act protects customers against false descriptions by those who are selling or providing services. The providing of services is interesting because it means that the Act applies in a wider context, to include things such as car hire. The Act does not require that there be an intention to deceive the customer, nor does it imply that anyone has actually been deceived.

As we have seen from R. v. Sunair Holidays Limited (1973) the descriptions have to be false at the time when they are made and cannot relate to the future. Wings Limited v. Ellis (1984) shows us that if a statement is correct at the time when it is made but circumstances then change, then a system must be set up to inform customers of the change. If such a system is not set up then offences continue to be committed as in R. v. Thomson Holidays (1974).

More Horror Stories

In 1981 Mr Wall booked a holiday from the Enterprise brochure at the Marina Apartotel in Puerto de la Cruz, Tenerife (Wall v. Silver Wing [1981]). During his holiday he suffered serious injury because a fire exit could not be used, as the door had been locked. It had in fact been locked by the hotel management to prevent burglars getting in, but Mr Wall claimed that he was entitled to presume that he would be safe in the hotel selected by the tour operator. Enterprise however responded by saying that the door was not locked when the hotel was inspected by their representative.

The judge decided in favour of the tour operator saying in effect that Enterprise could not be held responsible for the day-to-day running of the hotel. A tour operator is however obliged to *take care and attention* in selecting hotels and should carry out regular checks to satisfy themselves that they continue to be suitable for their clients.

A similar case, but this time with regard to transport, was heard in 1982 in Ontario, Canada (Craven v. Strand Holidays [1982]).

In this case the clients claimed damages because the bus in which they were travelling in Columbia, Canada overturned and they were injured. They claimed that the tour operator was responsible because the bus was booked through them.

Initially the trial judge found the tour operator guilty but on appeal it was decided that, as they had exercised *due care and attention* in selecting the bus company, they could not be held responsible for the accident to the bus.

Sale of Goods Act, 1979

This Act updated the original Sale of Goods Act of 1893. The Act applies to tour operators because they repackage accommodation and transport and sell ready-made holidays to the public. Tour operators are not simply acting as agents and, as the previous cases have shown, they must exercise due care and attention when selecting the elements of the holidays. Once tour operators have done this, they cannot be held responsible for the day-to-day running of the services that they have contracted. However, remembering Jarvis v. Swan Tours, tour operators should not be too glowing in their description of the services and should avoid giving what amounts to a guarantee of a good time.

Clients should understand the nature of what they are buying. If the holiday is a late availability one where clients leave the choice of hotel to the tour operator, the price of the holiday may be vastly reduced. However, clients should beware of imagining that the holiday will actually be of a higher standard than is described in the brochure. Similarly, the photograph of a swimming pool in the brochure will normally show the whole pool, and the client should be discouraged from imagining that it is only the corner of a larger pool!

On no account should the travel agent be responsible for misleading statements to clients by claiming to know resorts or hotels with which they are not, in fact, familiar.

Yet More Horror Stories

Another story (Jackson v. Horizon Holidays [1975]) which took place in Sri Lanka was that of Mr Jackson who booked an Horizon holiday for himself, his wife and their two children. The hotel was supposed to be of the highest standard and he requested a communicating door between the two bedrooms booked. Not only was there no communicating door, but the children's room was unusable due to mildew and fungus; there was a dirty shower rather than a bath as promised; and several hotel amenities, including the swimming pool, were non-existent.

Mr Jackson was successful in claiming substantial damages not only for himself, but also on behalf of his family, as his was the *lead name* on the booking form.

> The lead name is the first name on the booking form, and it is this person who should sign the booking form.

In 1980 a Mr Adcock was able to obtain damages for himself and a party of friends (Adcock v. Blue Sky [1980]).

In this case the party had booked a skiing holiday in Italy, but the standard of hygiene was very poor, the central heating intermittent and the general atmosphere and comfort of the hotel left a lot to be desired.

The trial judge awarded damages and when Blue Sky appealed, the appeal judge more than doubled the damages awarded because of the irritation, inconvenience and distress caused to all members of the party.

Supply of Goods and Services Act, 1982

This 1982 Act extended the protection of the Sale of Goods Act of 1979 to give greater protection not only to the buyer but also to those who hire or contract services. The goods and services should be up to an acceptable standard and fit for the purpose for which they are intended. The seller or provider should exercise 'reasonable care and skill' (Section 13) in providing the service.

As we saw from the two earlier stories, damages can be claimed for family and friends who holiday with a person who is not satisfied with the standard of service which is offered.

The implications of this Act for the tour operator are that:

♦ great care should be taken when selecting the accommodation or transport for the holidays;

♦ any services provided, such as that of a courier, should be of an acceptable standard.

The travel agent too should be careful when providing advice that such advice is of a professional standard. For instance, late availability cards displayed in the window should relate to holidays which can actually be booked.

◊ *Activity 9.2* ◊

During the year make your own collection of holiday horror stories. Try to analyse each case for the relevant facts and make a note of the outcome.
Note: the Sunday newspapers are usually a good source for such stories.

Criminal Offences and the Law of Torts

The Norman-French word **tort** simply means a wrong. In law in this country the word is used to identify wrongs which are serious enough to merit damages being awarded but which are not actually criminal offences.

> Serious wrongs, such as murder, are called crimes which are punished by the state. The offender is prosecuted in a criminal court by the Crown.
>
> On the other hand, the law of torts is to do with lesser wrongs which are not punished by the state, but where compensation is awarded in the form of damages. The injured party will have sued in a civil court.

Negligence

The modern tort of negligence stems from the famous case of Donoghue v. Stevenson (1932).

> Mrs Donoghue and a friend ordered a drink of ginger beer in a cafe in Paisley, near Glasgow. The drink came in an opaque glass bottle so the contents could not be seen. When Mrs Donoghue was in the process of pouring her second glass of ginger beer, out came the decomposed remains of a snail. Mrs Donoghue subsequently sued the manufacturer of the ginger beer who then claimed there was no contract between himself and Mrs Donoghue. However, the Law Lords ruled that there was a duty of care, which had been broken. Mrs Donoghue was unable to inspect the contents of the opaque bottle, but she was entitled to assume that its contents were fit for consumption.

Since that case it has been established that a consumer who wishes to claim for negligence has to prove three points:

♦ that the manufacturer owes him a duty of care;

♦ that the duty of care has been broken;

♦ that as a result, the consumer has suffered damage or injury.

We saw before that the client booking a package holiday must rely on the care of the tour operator and the travel agent. The average holiday-maker is not in a position to go and inspect the hotel abroad and must depend on the selection made by the tour operator and the advice offered by the travel agent.

Damages

Damages are awarded in civil cases in an attempt to compensate the person who has brought the complaint. There are two types of damages which can be awarded. These are special damages and general damages.

Special damages are easy to measure as they relate to out-of-pocket expenses. Out-of-pocket expenses might be incurred if, for example, telephone calls have to be made or alternative accommodation has to be found.

General damages are awarded as compensation for disappointment or mental stress and are more difficult to quantify. Compensation could range from a small amount to even double the original cost of the holiday as in Jarvis v. Swan Tours Limited [1973].

It is however unusual for the total cost of the holiday to be awarded as damages because it is difficult to prove that the client received no enjoyment whatsoever. Damages generally depend upon the importance of the lost facilities to the holiday. For instance, the lack of skis on a skiing holiday is drastic, but having to use the swimming pool in the hotel next door may not be regarded in the same category.

The court also considers whether:

♦ the client received any physical injuries, as in Wall v. Silver Wing (1981), or

♦ the client suffered mental stress and disappointment as in Jarvis v. Swan Tours Limited (1973).

The court will ask if the clients have attempted to mitigate their loss. This means, did they attempt to enjoy themselves and, if things went wrong, did they approach the tour representative to try to put things right?

I once saw a family who did not like their hotel in Torremolinos and insisted on sitting by the pool in their English heavyweight clothing in 90 degrees of heat rather than attempt to enjoy the holiday in any way. They could hardly be said to have mitigated their situation!

Ultimately the court will consider:

♦ the exact wording of the brochure which forms the basis of the contract with the client and

♦ the price paid for the holiday, as the price can be expected to reflect the quality being offered.

The Role of ABTA

ABTA's advice to the public in the event of things going wrong with a holiday is as follows.

♦ First that they should approach the tour representative or the hotel manager on the spot.

♦ If the matter cannot be resolved in this way, then the complaint should be recorded on the tour operator's official forms which will be available from the representative.

♦ On returning to the UK the client should then make the complaint known to their travel agent and tour operator.

♦ If the dispute cannot be resolved amicably, ABTA provides a free conciliation service or the use of their independent arbitration scheme.

A client wishing to use the **conciliation service** should write to ABTA enclosing:

♦ photocopies of any correspondence with the company involved,

♦ the confirmation invoice,

♦ any photographs or other evidence and

♦ an indication of what action is expected from the tour operator, whether it be an apology or some financial compensation.

The **arbitration scheme** offered by ABTA is run independently by the Chartered Institute of Arbitrators. It is

♦ cheap,

♦ concerned with written evidence only,

♦ available for up to nine months after the holiday.

It is not available for claims involving physical injury or illness. If clients choose to use the arbitration scheme, then this must be regarded as an alternative to going to court, as they must agree to abide by the decision of the arbitrators.

The Role of the Courts

England and Wales have the same legal system. Scotland and Northern Ireland each has its own legal system. Here we shall consider only the system for England and Wales, but similar information is readily available for the other systems.

When we noted the difference between the criminal law and the law of torts, we saw that there are criminal courts and civil courts. The majority of criminal prosecutions are brought first to a Magistrates Court. There is no jury in a Magistrates Court and there is a ceiling on the penalties which can be imposed. A person convicted in the Magistrates Court may be entitled to appeal against the decision to a higher court. The higher criminal courts are the Crown Court, the High Court, the Court of Appeal and the House of Lords.

Most civil actions are heard in the County Court over which presides a Circuit Court Judge. Again there are limits to the size of the claim which may be considered in this court. A person dissatisfied with the verdict in the County Court can appeal to the High Court where jurisdiction is unlimited. Appeals can still be taken to the Court of Appeal and ultimately to the House of Lords.

For those who do not wish to embark on what could be a costly court case there also exists the 'small claims procedure' which comes within the County Court. This is a form of arbitration where the claim must come below a certain limit. The cost is reasonable, but neither side may claim their legal costs. This procedure is popular for smaller claims such as complaints about holidays where the amount of compensation being sought is relatively small.

Diagram 9.3 (page 132) summarises the earlier points with regard to offences, courts and possible outcomes. Activity 9.3 (page 132) will give you an opportunity to establish the current levels of costs, fines, punishments and compensations.

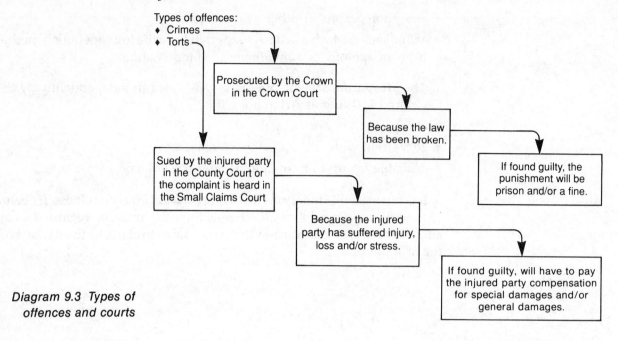

Types of offences:
♦ Crimes
♦ Torts

Prosecuted by the Crown
in the Crown Court

Because the law
has been broken.

Sued by the injured party
in the County Court or
the complaint is heard in
the Small Claims Court

If found guilty, the
punishment will be
prison and/or a fine.

Because the injured
party has suffered injury,
loss and/or stress.

If found guilty, will have to pay
the injured party compensation
for special damages and/or
general damages.

*Diagram 9.3 Types of
offences and courts*

◇ *Activity 9.3* ◇

Make a visit to a Magistrates, Crown and/or High Court. By questioning officials at the courts and/or visiting the local library or Citizens' Advice Bureau find the current values for the following.

1 What is the maximum fine which can be imposed in a Magistrates Court?

2 What is the maximum prison sentence which can be imposed in a Magistrates Court?

3 What is the maximum amount which can be claimed in a County Court for breach of contract?

4 What is the maximum amount which can be claimed in the 'small claims procedure' of the County Court?

5 What is the cost of taking a case to the 'small claims procedure'?

The Role of the Travel Agent when Problems Arise

Whatever the client's complaint, the travel agent is very likely to be their first line of approach and the agent should remember that they have two major roles to play.

♦ The first role is that of the client's own agent who is prepared to listen, sympathise and advise as to whether or not there seems to be genuine cause for complaint.

♦ The second role is that of agent for the tour operator.

The travel agent's place is not to take sides in a dispute but simply to take an impartial view and advise an appropriate course of action.

◊ *Revision Questions* ◊

1 If Mr Walsh goes into a travel agency, Trendy Travel, and books a holiday from the Happy Holidays brochure, with whom does he make a contract?

2 Name the three ways in which a contract may be made.

3 Where will your client find details of compensation for any changes made by the tour operator to a holiday after it has been booked?

4 Which Act of Parliament protects the public against a tour operator including misleading descriptions in a brochure?

5 How should a tour operator select accommodation or transport?

6 Crimes are punished by the state, but what will be the outcome of a successful action for an offence in tort?

7 If a client wishes to claim negligence, which three points need to be proved?

8 If a client wishes to complain that the hotel facilities are inferior to the standard described in the brochure, what is the first action that should be taken?

9 Name the service which ABTA offers, if a complaint cannot be resolved between a client and a tour operator.

10 In some circumstances the ABTA Code of Conduct allows tour operators to make changes to a holiday without being obliged to compensate the client. Give one example of such a situation.

10 *Cruising*

By the end of this chapter you should have increased your:

♦ knowledge of types of cruises and destinations;
♦ skills in advising clients who have queries about their cruising holidays and life on board ship.

Cruising can be regarded as the ultimate package holiday in a floating hotel. All arrangements are made for the client.

♦ The cruise ship provides all meals, twenty-four hours a day, from a sumptuous breakfast to a midnight feast.

♦ Cabins vary in size and decor, but a cabin and table steward are assigned to each person with a ratio of one crew member to every two passengers on the more luxurious ships.

♦ The public entertaining rooms offer a choice of bars and restaurants, as well as facilities such as a ballroom, a fitness centre, a cinema and a casino.

♦ The total relaxation and variety of ports of call are said to be addictive to some people, and cruise companies claim a high percentage of repeat bookings.

There is a very lucrative market here for the travel agent because, with the high prices involved, the commission can be very worthwhile. In this chapter we will consider:

♦ cruise ships;

♦ types of cruises;

♦ facilities on board;

♦ advice which could be offered by the travel agent to clients who are cruising for the first time;

♦ some destinations of cruises.

Cruise Ships

In Chapter Two we saw a little of the history of ocean-going liners and their demise in the 1960s with the coming of the wide bodied jet aeroplanes. Companies such as Cunard and P & O responded to this demise by using the *QE2* and *Canberra* as cruise ships rather than liners. In this way they could take a group of passengers to a number of ports, usually in the Mediterranean or the Canaries, and then back to the UK, all within a specific time ranging from ten days to a few weeks. With the success of these cruises, other companies commissioned purpose-built ships.

For example in 1972 the Royal Viking Line introduced *Royal Viking Star* which not only took fewer passengers than either the *QE2* or *Canberra* but also had a lower **density**. The density is a means by which we can measure the space available on a ship in relation to each passenger.

Each ship has its Gross Registered Tonnage (GRT), a figure which indicates the size of the ship. The GRT can be found in manuals such as the *ABC Passenger Shipping Guide*. The Guide also gives the maximum number of passengers on the ship. For the *QE2* the GRT is 66 450 tons and it carries 1877 passengers. If we divide the GRT of the vessel by the number of passengers we arrive at the density of the ship. So:

66 450 divided by 1877 gives a density of 35

For *Canberra*, the GRT is 43 975 and it carries 1706 passengers, giving a density of 25. This measurement of density shows that the passengers on *QE2* have more space to themselves than those on *Canberra*. In general a higher figure, and therefore lower density, can be taken as an indication of larger cabins, more deck space and less crowded restaurants.

The *Royal Viking Star* which was purpose-built in 1972 carried only 700 passengers with a GRT of 28 221 giving a very low density of 40. The following year a sister ship, the *Royal Viking Sky* was built with an even lower density of 56. This trend to more spacious cruise ships continues with the Japanese company Nippon Yusen Kaisha ordering a cruise ship of 50 000 tons to be built by Mitsubishi to carry 960 passengers. This gives a low density of 52, about twice as spacious as *Canberra*.

◇ *Activity 10.1* ◇

Calculating the density is one method which helps when appreciating the differences between cruise ships. On the basis of the GRT and the number of passengers carried, which of the following ships would possibly offer your client more space and comfort?

1 *Sovereign of the Seas*, built for Royal Carribean Cruise Line as a floating resort with a GRT of 70 000 tons carrying 2276 passengers.

2 *Ocean Islander* which carries only 260 passengers and advertises 'a world of yacht-like cruising'. This Ocean Cruise Liners ship has a GRT of 5000 tons.

3 Royal Viking Line's ship the *Royal Viking Sun*, which was introduced into service in January 1989 with a GRT of 36 000, over a third larger than previous ships in the Line, and carrying 740 passengers.

4 The Sun Line Cruises *Stella Maris* with a GRT of 2682 tons carrying only 200 passengers on an 'experience of a lifetime' around Italy.

Types of Cruises

The cruise market worldwide is approximately three million passengers with about 80 per cent of these being from North America. To sell cruise holidays, the travel agent must appreciate the sort of person who will take a cruise. Traditionally in the UK, cruising has had an upmarket image thought to appeal to the older generation and to be too expensive for the average holidaymaker. Cruise companies now realise that this image is changing and have introduced:

♦ entertainment for younger clientele;

♦ facilities for children, in order to attract families;

♦ flights out to cruise areas to reduce the time spent actually reaching warmer climes.

At a normal speed, cruise ships can do an average of 400 to 500 miles in a twenty-four hour period. This speed means that the traditional **port to port** cruises from the UK to the Mediterranean can spend two or three days each way in the Bay of Biscay, an area renowned for poor weather conditions. To avoid this and take the client as quickly as possible to their desired area **fly/cruises** have been introduced. With fly/cruises the Mediterranean is more accessible and ports such as Miami and Fort Lauderdale in Florida have become major home ports for Caribbean cruising. Over 40 per cent of UK passengers taking cruises start their holiday with a flight.

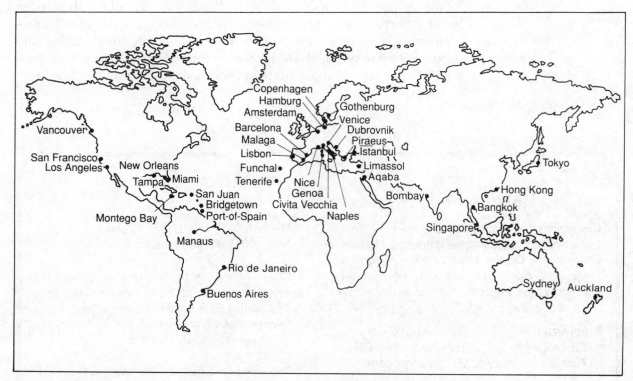

Diagram 10.1 World map showing fly/cruise ports

Fly/cruise holidays are sometimes combined with hotel accommodation for a period of time making the **cruise and stay** holiday. It is possible to fly out to Florida, spend a week in Orlando seeing Disney World and other attractions and then join a cruise from Miami to the Caribbean for a second week.

For clients with more available time, there are round the world cruises. These are offered by a number of companies, including Cunard, P & O and CTC with visits to the Far East, India, South Africa and North or South America.

Realising that potential clients for cruising are very varied, Cunard and P & O try to offer different images through different brochures. Offering different brochures in this way is called **market segmentation** and this will be studied in more detail in Chapter Eleven. Cunard have bought the Scandinavian ships *Vistafjord* and *Sagafjord* which they describe as 'the world's only five star plus sister ships' and attract a different clientele from that which traditionally cruises on *QE2*. Likewise *Canberra* still provides an excellent cruising holiday but the P & O Princess Voyages appeal to the upper end of the market.

In the United States cruising is being marketed to younger people. Carnival Cruise Line claims an average age of 35 on their Fun Ships. Cheaper prices, a change in entertainment and the influence of the TV series *Love Boat* are all said to have contributed to this change of image.

Facilities On Board

Diagram 10.2 is from the Royal Caribbean Cruises' brochure and shows the layout of the *M/S Sun Viking*.

♦ The side view diagram shows the decks in relation to each other.

♦ The other diagrams show the positions of facilities and cabins on each deck.

It is useful to notice that:

♦ decks on ships are referred to as A Deck, not Deck A;

♦ some decks have names which are indicative of the activities on the deck, such as Restaurant Deck;

♦ public rooms for entertainment are on separate decks from the cabins;

♦ the higher the number or letter of the deck, the lower it is in the ship.

The front of the ship is known as the bow or fore, while the back of the ship is the stern or aft. Looking forward

♦ the left hand side of the ship is the port side and it has a red navigational light and

♦ the right side is starboard and it has a green navigational light.

> The easy way to remember port and starboard is that the words *port* and *left* both have four letters, and port wine is red in colour, the same as the port navigational light.

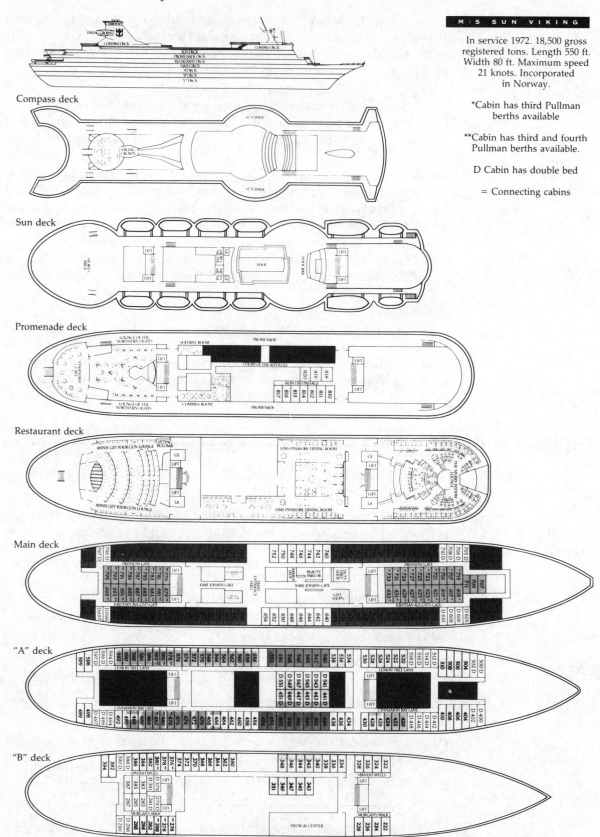

M/S SUN VIKING

In service 1972. 18,500 gross
registered tons. Length 550 ft.
Width 80 ft. Maximum speed
21 knots. Incorporated
in Norway.

*Cabin has third Pullman
berths available

**Cabin has third and fourth
Pullman berths available.

D Cabin has double bed

= Connecting cabins

Compass deck

Sun deck

Promenade deck

Restaurant deck

Main deck

"A" deck

"B" deck

*Diagram 10.2 Layout of
M/S Sun Viking*

Cabins are sometimes referred to as staterooms and these vary in size and price according to where they are in the ship. The more expensive cabins, referred to as penthouses or deluxe suites, are usually on the higher decks and have their own bathrooms and even lounge areas. The cheapest cabins are usually on the lower decks and may have only a hand basin with shared facilities for toilets and showers.

Another factor which influences price is whether or not the cabin has a porthole or window. Those with a porthole or window are known as outside cabins and those without natural light are referred to as inside cabins. Inside cabins are cheaper.

> On *Canberra*, P & O have an ingenious design shown in Diagram 10.3. These court cabins are built so that each of six cabins has a corner window receiving light from a large window at the end of the court. The arrangement gives two three-berth, two two-bedded and two single cabins in a group. This can be useful for families or groups of friends who wish to book adjacent cabins.

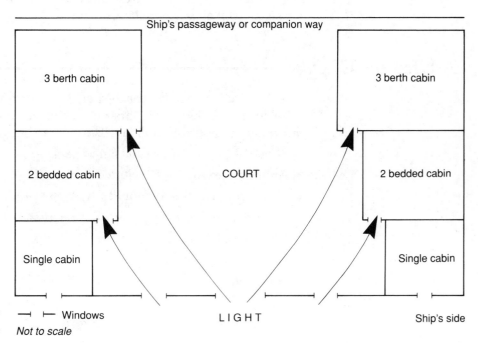

Diagram 10.3 Court cabins

The beds in cabins are sometimes called berths but it is important to understand the terminology when booking a cabin.

♦ A two-bedded cabin will have two beds, just as a hotel room might have twin beds.

♦ A two-berth cabin will have two beds arranged on top of each other like bunk beds.

♦ Some ships offer large two-bedded cabins which have foldaway berths above. These are good for families with children.

♦ Not all ships have single cabins, and with some companies it may be necessary to pay quite a large supplement to have the use of a two-berth or two-bedded cabin for single occupancy.

♦ Deck plans show which rooms have interconnecting doors.

Facilities on board usually include:

♦ sports and recreation such as deck-tennis, shuffleboard, quoits,
♦ fitness centre or gym,
♦ jogging tracks around the deck,
♦ swimming pools,
♦ sunbathing areas,
♦ selection of bars,
♦ restaurants,
♦ shops,
♦ night club,
♦ casino,
♦ cinema,
♦ ballroom,
♦ laundry,
♦ hairdressing and beauty salon,
♦ libraries,
♦ card room,
♦ computer room,
♦ medical centre which will be a mini hospital with a qualified doctor on all cruises.

The entertainment is organised by the Cruise Director or Entertainments Officer and a programme for the day is placed in each cabin every morning. There is of course no compulsion to join in the activities. Not all ships encourage children, but those who do, provide a play room and nurse, as well as reasonable reductions.

Advice for Clients

The most important advice is the help the client may require in choosing a suitable cruise. However, first-time cruisers may want more detailed information about the holiday. Typical worries include:

♦ Should I take cash or travellers cheques?

♦ Are shore excursions included in the price?

♦ Who, and how much should I tip?

♦ What happens if I am ill during the cruise?

♦ What should I wear?

♦ What is included in the price?

♦ How and when will I receive the ticket?

Should I Take Cash or Travellers Cheques?

Clients can be advised that the Cruise Office or the Purser's Office will be their main source of information for any everyday enquiries. The cruise office provides the following services:

♦ post office and bank;

♦ safety deposit boxes;

♦ exchange of cash or travellers cheques;

♦ ship-to-shore radio or telephone by satellite;

♦ the handling of all documentation at ports of call, including landing cards and liaison with the immigration and port police.

The currency used on board will be mentioned in the brochure and it is often the currency of the home port, but frequently American dollars are used. Major credit cards are accepted on most cruises, although not for obtaining cash or paying bar bills.

Are Shore Excursions Included in the Price?

Most ships have a Shore Excursion Office and clients can be advised that shore excursions are optional and usually involve extra cost. For first-timers they are probably the best way to make full use of the hours in port because coaches will be waiting to take passengers on trips which have been well-organised in advance. The brochure will give details of the number of hours to be spent in port and for any smaller ports it will indicate if the passengers have to go ashore by **tender**. Tender means using a small boat, very often utilising the life boats, to ferry from the ship to the quayside.

Some brochures give information about ports of call with the itinerary and prices, others give the details in a separate section or booklet.

Who and How Much Should I Tip?

Clients sometimes worry about not knowing who is who in the crew. They can be assured that they will be assigned a cabin steward as well as a restaurant or table steward who will look after them throughout the cruise. Royal Caribbean Cruise Line have produced an excellent video called *Behind the Scenes* which describes the work done by the crew during a cruise.

Tipping is a worry for some first-timers and they can be told that:

◆ where drinks are signed for at the bar, a 10 per cent or sometimes 15 per cent service charge or tip is automatically added to the bill;

◆ tipping for the cabin and table stewards is at the client's discretion;

◆ a figure of 10 per cent of the cost of the cruise would be an indication of what could be divided between these stewards.

What Happens if I am Ill During the Cruise?

All major cruise lines provide a medical doctor on board and the facilities in the mini-hospital are usually excellent. However, clients should be advised that:

◆ the treatment in these centres does not come under the National Health Service;

◆ they should have adequate medical insurance cover;

◆ passengers over the age of 75 are required by some companies to have a certificate of fitness to travel when they book their cruise;

◆ any physical disabilities should be notified before sailing;

◆ although wheelchairs are accepted on cruises, only a limited number will be allowed on any particular cruise.

What Should I Wear?

With regard to dress, advice is sometimes given in the brochure. In general it is safe to say that the client will need casual clothing for daytime and more formal wear for the evening. The more expensive and luxurious the cruise, the more likelihood of using a dinner jacket and cocktail dresses, but all cruises will have at least a few occasions when passengers are invited to dress in style. Fancy dress parties are also part of the programme for those who wish to participate.

What is Included in the Price?

As with ordinary package holidays, the brochure will list what is included in the price of the cruise. The total price usually covers:

♦ all meals on board,

♦ all entertainment on board,

♦ port charges,

♦ the flight out and back on fly/cruises,

♦ free car-parking at the port, when this is offered,

♦ subsidised travel to the port, when this is offered.

When filling in the booking form, great care should be taken to complete all details accurately. Correct information will need to be given for

♦ the cruise number,

♦ the cabins required,

♦ decks required,

♦ preferred meal times,

♦ preferred table size,

♦ preferred company at the table,

♦ insurance,

♦ any extras such as subsidised travel.

Diagram 10.4 shows the booking form for Royal Caribbean Cruises and some of the requests for details are highlighted. Information about the passport number and nationality of the client are required for immigration purposes.

How and When Will I Receive the Ticket?

About twelve weeks before departure the client will receive an information pack which will include the ticket, details of checking-in times for the cruise or flight and details of the proposed disembarkation or return time. The disembarkation time cannot be given with complete accuracy but clients can expect to leave a ship approximately two hours after it reaches the home port.

Your guide around paradise

ROYAL CARIBBEAN ⚓ CRUISES

Bishops Palace House, 2A Riverside Walk, Kingston-uponThames KT1 1QN
Tel: Reservations 01-541 5044. Administration 01-541 5570. Telex: 261383 RCCL G. Prestel: 53317. Fax: 01-546 8803. 1st Edition.

BOOKING FORM 1989 (1st Edition)	**BOOKING NO:**
Holiday No. _____ RCCL Ref. _____	*Dining Room Sitting: Smoking ☐ Non-Smoking ☐
Ship _____	Main: Breakfast 7.30 am, Lunch 12.00 noon, Dinner 6.30pm ☐
Dep. ex London _____	Second: Breakfast 8.45 am, Lunch 1.30pm, Dinner 8.30 pm ☐
Free Domestic Flights _____	Preferred table size: 4 ☐ 6 ☐ 8 ☐ 10 ☐
Sailing Date _____	Preferred Age Group: 18-30 ☐ 31-45 ☐ 46-60 ☐ 61+ ☐
Additional Flight Arrangements _____	Have you cruised with RCCL before? Yes ☐ No ☐
Cabin Category _____ Cabin No. _____	Insurance Yes ☐ No ☐

ADDITIONAL HOLIDAY/U.S. FLIGHT ARRANGEMENTS

Holiday No.	Date Commencing	Hotel	Number of Nights	Accomodation

Car hire		Date Commencing	No. of Days	Grade

PASSENGER DETAILS

Mr/Mrs/Miss	Surname	Christian name	Birth Date	Nationality	Passport No.	Visa No.

Home Address
_____
_____
_____

Home Tel. No. _____

Business Tel. No. _____

Special Requests
_____
_____
_____

In case of an emergency please notify

Name _____

Address _____

Tel. No. _____

Please complete either

Deposit (£100 per person) × _____	= £ _____
Insurance (£35 per person) × _____	= £ _____
Total amount enclosed	= £ _____

or (Price Pledge detailed on page 45)

Full price of holiday © £ _____	= £ _____
Insurance (£35 per person) × _____	= £ _____
Total amount enclosed	= £ _____

Agents stamp

Blundellsands Travel
38 Bridge Road
Blundellsands
Liverpool _____

Abta No. _____   Agents ref. _____

SIGNED _____   Date _____

I agree on behalf of all persons named in this Booking Form to be bound by the Booking Conditions stated below and the insurance held warranty overleaf.
*Although every attempt will be made to satisfy your client's request, please be advised that all dining room seating arrangements are subject to availability and prior assignment. No arrangements will be made until receipt of final payment.

*Diagram 10.4 Royal
Caribbean Cruises
booking form*

◇ *Activity 10.2* ◇

This activity could be done while you are on work placement and have access to a selection of brochures.

Collect together the current brochures for the following cruise lines and then answer the ten questions below using each brochure.

You will need these brochures again for Activity 11.2 when we consider market segmentation.

- Cunard's *QE2* programme
- P & O's *Canberra* programme
- Royal Caribbean Cruises
- CTC Cruises
- Equity Cruises

1 Is there any free or subsidised travel to the port of departure?

2 Are the major destinations Mediterranean, Baltic or Caribbean?

3 Is there any limit to the baggage a passenger may take?

4 Will the client need a visa for any of the cruises in the brochure?

5 Are there set meal times? If so, what are they?

6 Is there a fitness centre or gym?

7 What is the currency used on board ship?

8 Are credit cards accepted? Are there any limits to their use?

9 What voltage of electricity is used on board?

10 Is it possible to send letters from the ship?

Destinations of Cruises

Apart from round the world cruises, the most popular destinations are the Mediterranean, the Baltic and the Caribbean. Round-the-world cruises are available with CTC and P & O. The minimum price for a world cruise is about £5000, with prices on P & O's *Canberra* rising to over £29 000 and those on CTC's *Azerbaydzhan* rising to about £16 000.

Both ships take a west to east route around the world, calling at Mediterranean ports, travelling through the Suez Canal and on to Singapore and Australia. Both return to Europe through the Panama Canal and the Caribbean. The CTC cruise also takes in India and Sri Lanka and the P & O cruise includes Hawaii and San Francisco.

It is possible to cruise in sectors on any of the world cruises by flying out to join the ship for a period of time and taking in the ports of call of one specific area.

Mediterranean Cruises

Mediterranean cruises generally stay either in the western Mediterranean or in the eastern Mediterranean, but *Canberra* cruises the length of the Mediterranean from Southampton a few times a year. *Canberra's* UK to the Mediterranean cruises take a minimum of 16 days and prices start from under £1000. Other cruises from the UK to the Mediterranean only go as far as Corsica or Italy. Such cruises are offered from the ports of Southampton, by *Canberra* and the *QE2*, and Tilbury by CTC.

Some cruises from the UK cover areas of the Mediterranean while concentrating on Madeira and the Canaries. *Canberra*, *QE2* and CTC all offer these, as well as *Black Prince* of the Fred Olsen Line. Prices for these cruises start at around £800. Cruises to the western Mediterranean are a little more expensive than those to the Canaries.

If clients wish to cruise the Greek islands or the Middle East then they will usually start with a flight to Athens or Venice. In spite of the cost of the flight, these cruises can be done for about the same price as those out of the UK ports. Clients should beware, however, of a few cruises which do not include the cost of the flight.

> Cruises to the Mediterranean are available from May to October whilst those to the Canaries tend to be in Spring or Autumn.

Baltic Cruises

Baltic cruises are also available from May to October and include ports in Norway, Sweden, Denmark and Russia. Many Baltic cruises are offered in the period from the middle of June to the first week in July. At this time of the year it is possible to see the midnight sun in the most northerly regions. The midnight sun occurs during the few short weeks from late June when the sun shines continually both night and day in the far north. This, combined with the spectacular scenery of the fjords, can make an unforgettable sight.

The two major companies operating in the Baltic are Scandinavian Seaways out of Harwich and CTC out of Tilbury. *Canberra* and *QE2* each do a single trip at the time of the midnight sun and these depart from Southampton. Prices vary a great deal with CTC offering the cheapest cruises at £700, P & O's *Canberra* at just under £900 and Cunard's *QE2* at over £1300.

Itineraries also vary but most will include:

♦ ancient cities such as Copenhagen with the Tivoli Gardens, and Leningrad with the Hermitage and the Tsar's palace at Petrodvorets;

♦ northerly towns such as Narvik and Trondheim, the former Norwegian capital;

♦ beautiful fjords such as Hardangerfjord and Gierangerefjord with their steep cliff faces and waterfalls.

Caribbean Cruises

Caribbean cruises are offered all year round and usually involve a flight to join the ship. Most flights are from London but Ocean Cruise Lines also offers flights from Manchester. Some of the most popular cruise lines operating in the area are Equity, Norwegian Cruise Line and Royal Caribbean Cruises. The most popular home ports are Miami in Florida, San Juan in Puerto Rico, Fort Lauderdale, Port Everglades and the islands of St Thomas or Barbados.

Excluding the flight time, cruises can take from three days to a fortnight and itineraries can be equally varied. All destinations offer the traditional palm trees, sand and sun but in addition there are a wealth of different cultures to be sampled. St John's, Antigua and Bridgetown, Barbados have their English connections. Ocho Rios in Jamaica offers a genuine Caribbean atmosphere as well as the beautiful Dunn's River Falls where the roaring cascades make a refreshing change from endless white sands. In Martinique the citizens enjoy full French citizenship. At St Maarten the jewels and watches for sale remind one of their Dutch heritage.

While the Mediterranean, the Baltic and the Caribbean are the most popular areas for cruising from this country, they are not the only available areas. Cruises are regularly offered:

- across the Atlantic, taking in the Canaries or Barbados, and calling at Caribbean resorts before arriving in New York or New Orleans;
- right around South America and such cruises are on a par with round the world cruises, as they can take from forty to fifty days for the full trip;
- in the far north by the Exploration Cruise Line with the ships *Great River Explorer* and *North Star*. These ships ply the waters off Canada and Alaska through the beautiful fjords between Ketchikan and Skagway.

Summary

Cruising is a special kind of holiday which is appealing to more and more people.

The destinations and ships are varied enough to attract a large section of the public.

The Passenger Shipping Association is currently involved in a nationwide training programme for retail travel agents (PSARA) and they produce magazines and seminars to help the travel agent give up-to-date, accurate information on cruises to the public.

Cruising is probably one of the greatest potential growth markets in the travel business today.

◊ *Revision Questions* ◊

1 List four ports of call which could be included on a Mediterranean cruise.

2 List four ports of call which could be included on a Caribbean cruise.

3 What is the difference between a two-bedded cabin and a two-berth cabin?

4 List four facilities which would be included in the cost of a cruise.

5 If a ship has a Gross Registered Tonnage of 25 000 and carries 500 passengers, what is its density?

6 Would you describe the ship in question 5 as spacious or not? Give a reason for your answer.

7 List four types of sporting activities which could be offered on a cruise.

8 List four quieter pursuits which could be followed on a cruise.

9 What advice would you give to a client with regard to tipping on a cruise?

10 What do you understand by the term 'the port of embarkation'?

11 *Travel Marketing Skills*

By the end of this chapter you should have increased your:

♦ **knowledge of the marketing mix, or the four Ps, the life cycle of holidays, market segmentation and marketing research methods;**

♦ **skills in analysing travel promotions, recognising market segmentation in brochures and conducting a survey.**

What is Marketing?

Marketing is all about:

♦ knowing and understanding the needs of your customers,

♦ creating the right product to satisfy those needs and

♦ letting the customers know that you have just what they want.

It sounds simple, but a great deal of research has to go into:

♦ knowing the customer,

♦ identifying the needs,

♦ getting the product right, and

♦ getting the product to the right customer.

Marketing is concerned with all of these activities.

There is no profit to be made in producing a product which nobody wants. Neither is there any profit in producing the right product but failing to let people know about it. Sometimes a need is an obvious one, as in basic necessities such as food and water, but sometimes a basic need can be refined by a good marketing team so that the customer comes to desire a particular food or even a particular brand of food.

The same is true of holidays. There may be a general feeling of wanting to get away for a rest, or simply going somewhere different. In Chapter Two we have already considered the reasons people give for taking holidays and, as we saw, these can be quite numerous. In fact, the same person may actually take a holiday for a variety of reasons. That person may be visiting friends or relatives but at the same time he or she may wish to see some of the historical places of interest in an area. Another person may be going on a religious pilgrimage but may also wish to take a few days relaxing in another environment. The shrine of Lourdes in France attracts many pilgrims and a fair number of them combine the pilgrimage with a further week in the resort of San Sebastian in northern Spain.

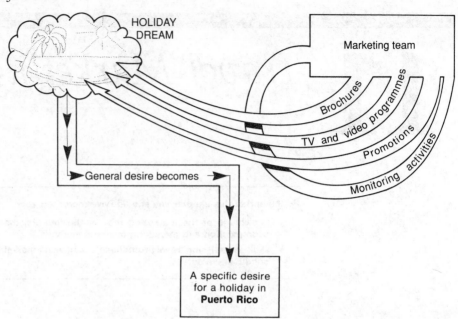

Diagram 11.1 The role of the marketing team

It is the marketing team's job to identify areas where they can help the client to see a general need or want, as a specific desire for the product offered by the team's company. A marketing team takes into account what is known as the marketing mix or the four **Ps**. These are:

♦ **Product**   ♦ **Price**
♦ **Place**   ♦ **Promotion**

In the travel industry the **product** can be

♦ a package tour,
♦ an independent holiday,
♦ a ferry crossing,
♦ an airline journey,
♦ car hire,
♦ day excursions or
♦ a hotel.

With regard to the product, the company must look at:

♦ the design and quality of existing products,
♦ the possibilities of new products and
♦ the products of competitors.

Sometimes tour operators delay the launch of their brochures in order to see what the opposition has to offer.

Some tour operators issue fresh editions of the brochure in response to competition. In fact, new editions have become so much part of the travel scene that the larger tour operators no longer publish prices in the main brochure, but put them in an inset booklet which is simple to reprint.

Possible future products must always be under consideration if the company is not to become complacent and stagnant and all the features of the product should be reviewed regularly.

A holiday is an intangible product, meaning something that cannot be touched or experienced by the client until they have actually bought it. If a customer is buying a car or a coat they would expect to be able to try it before parting with their money. However, a holiday in Spain has to be taken based on the description in the brochure.

There is inevitably an element of risk attached to buying any intangible product and the client is dependent on the description given by the brochure and the advice offered by the travel agent. It is not without good reason that principals send their sales representatives around travel agencies to make sure that their brochures are adequately and suitably displayed. Some principals prefer to sell direct to the public but this makes them even more dependent on the accuracy, wide distribution and availability of their brochure. Furthermore, the holiday is also dependent on the quality of service received by the client during the holiday and the tour operator cannot have control over the personality of the waiter at a hotel or indeed the weather, should it prove to be unseasonal.

The **place** is very important in travel because we are concerned with:

♦ sending clients to the right holiday destination, and

♦ sending clients from the right departure point.

The holiday destination should be suitable for the client and popular enough to produce profit for the principal. The departure point might be an airport, a local railway station or a coach pick-up point.

The **price**, or the cost to the customer, must be carefully calculated, as we saw in Chapter Eight. In calculating the cost, tour operators, airlines and other principals must also take into account:

♦ fixed costs,	♦ discounts,
♦ variable costs,	♦ surcharges and
♦ profit,	♦ commission for agents.

The current price at which a similar product is being sold by competitors is also a very relevant factor.

Discount, or cheap, pricing can lead to fierce competition between the main tour operators, with prices being cut to an absolute minimum in order to retain business. However, the lessons of the Court Line collapse in 1974, which was described in Chapter Two, should have taught the UK travel trade to beware of too much price cutting which can herald bankruptcy for some companies.

Premium or high pricing depends on the quality of the product and the perceptions of the customers. There is a growing tendency for the UK travel trade to consider the upper end of the market as the most important, with more expensive, long haul holidays being packaged and sold.

Later we shall consider market segmentation and how brochures can be aimed at particular customers. Whether considering discount or premium pricing, the tour operator must be sure that the price is acceptable to the potential customers.

Finally, **promotion** is the means by which the customer is told of the product and its price. This can be achieved by advertising and selling, which are the main or primary promotional forces. Also important are sales promotions and public relations which are the secondary forces.

Advertising, or making the holiday known to the public, may be found in newspapers, on the radio and/or on television. Travel agents sometimes share the cost of newspaper advertising with principals.

Wherever advertising is used it should comply with the accepted standards and controls of the relevant public bodies such as the Advertising Standards Authority (ASA) which relates to the written word, or the Independent Broadcasting Authority (IBA) which relates to advertising broadcasts on radio and television.

Selling is the main activity and reason for the existence of travel agencies. Until a holiday is actually sold the travel agent does not earn commission, which is their main source of income. Selling in a travel agency is dealt with in more detail in Chapter Thirteen.

Sales promotions are events organised to attract attention to the product or holiday on offer. Tour operators sometimes have a promotional evening for travel agents when they launch a new brochure. During the evening:

♦ the travel agents will be shown copies of the brochure which they are encouraged to take home;

♦ there may be a video or talk about the destinations featured in the brochure;

♦ there will usually be a buffet served in comfortable hotel surroundings;

♦ the buffet may be followed by a disco or cabaret act to round off the evening.

Travel agents in their turn hold promotional evenings to attract the attention of the public. January and February are usually a good time for travel agents to organise their own promotional days or evenings, which are very often in hotels or conference rooms. January and February are a good time for travel agents' promotions because people are more likely to be bored in the winter. They welcome the chance of an evening in a hotel watching videos and receiving maybe a free drink as well as pens, T-shirts and of course the latest holiday brochure. It is very likely that one of your own local travel agents will organise such a promotion and it would be excellent experience if you could offer your services as a guide or host for the event.

Many of the larger companies use their brand name or logo to promote a **corporate image** through products ranging from scarves to pens, and from mugs to travel bags. A corporate image means that the public will associate the company with the symbol or even the colour which is used in that company's promotions and advertising.

Companies like City Travel Trade Supplies print and produce numerous promotional products for some of the larger companies such as British Airways and Saga Holidays, as well as catering for small orders from independent companies. Brand names and logos can be a very powerful aid to marketing and selling.

> Marks and Spencer, for instance, have built up a reputation for quality and reliability which enables them to branch out into areas other than selling merchandise. Thus Marks and Spencer now sell not only clothes and food but also furnishings, furniture and even their own insurance. They still retain the loyalty and trust of their regular customers in the new venture because they know they can depend on the very name of Marks and Spencer.

In the same way the larger tour operators use their brand name and logos to promote a variety of brochures. Examine the range of Thomson brochures and see how the layout and titles incorporate the same image to reassure a client who has booked a holiday in the past, that any other Thomson holiday will have the same good standard.

Travel agents too can build on their past reputation by using their name or logo consistently. The larger multiples such as Thomas Cook and Lunn Poly do this, even through the decor of their shops and uniform of their staff. A small independent travel agent can use the name of their agency in promotions and sponsorship of local charity events, to help the public to associate their name with quality and excellence.

Whatever means are used for promoting the holiday or product the aims of the promotion can be summed up as they are in Diagram 11.2. Marketing experts agree that there are four stages of response by consumers to a product, and promotions should make use of these stages. AIDA is a well known way of remembering that the promotion should attract *Attention*, arouse *Interest*, create a *Desire* and stimulate *Action*. Activity 11.1 will help you to see AIDA in action.

Stages in promoting a product

Attract	**A**ttention
Arouse	**I**nterest
Create a	**D**esire
Stimulate	**A**ction

Diagram 11.2

Public relations means the way by which the company keeps in touch with customers and deals with any problems or complaints. In Chapter Seven we considered the role of a tour operator's customer service department. This is the department which deals with public relations. Such activities are equally important in a travel agency, whether it be a large multiple or a smaller independent. Without the goodwill and interest of the public none of these companies can remain in business. Chapter Thirteen gives some hints for dealing with difficult or irate customers in a travel agency.

◇ *Activity 11.1* ◇

Take part in a promotional evening as suggested on page 150 or, if this is not possible, make a collection of travel agents' advertisements from the local press.

Whichever activity you choose to do, analyse the promotion in terms of AIDA. List the means used. The following questions will help you.

1 How is attention brought to the advertisement or event? For example, is the design of the advertisement particularly eye-catching?

2 How is interest aroused? For example, is there some kind of free gift or free draw at the event?

3 Is a desire being created? For example, what kind of holiday is being emphasised?

4 Is any action being prompted? For example, is there a special discount for holidays booked at the promotional event?

Analyse the event or advertisements and try to arrange an interview with the travel agent to discuss the strategy and approach to the event or advertisement. Use the opportunity to discuss other successful promotions organised by the agency in the past.

The Product Life Cycle in Marketing

Many products seem to follow a similar pattern, known as the product life cycle, of three stages. These are:

♦ introduction,

♦ followed by acceptance on the part of the customers and

♦ finally a decline in popularity.

Diagram 11.3 shows the relationship between the product life cycle and profits when launching a package holiday brochure.

A package holiday in a brochure follows this cycle from its production, which, as we saw in Diagram 8.1 (page 113), will begin eighteen months or two years ahead of the launch, through to a few weeks before departure

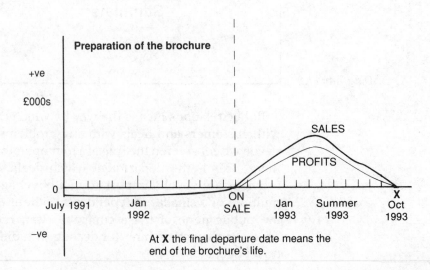

Diagram 11.3 Product life cycle of a summer 1993 brochure

At **X** the final departure date means the end of the brochure's life.

when the last seats are sold off cheaply as late availability. The diagram shows the product life cycle of a summer brochure for 1993.

♦ Production begins in July 1991.

♦ For the next 18 months the tour operator must cover all costs.

♦ Once the brochure goes on sale, profits are made in proportion to the number of sales, with the peak sales and profits coming around April or May 1993.

♦ As the summer season finishes, and the last availability is sold from the brochure, the package holiday and the profits all cease in October 1993.

Diagram 11.4 shows the product life cycle of a holiday destination as an ongoing product which the company may wish to offer year after year.

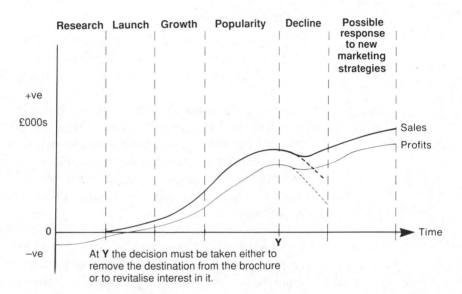

Diagram 11.4 Product life cycle of a holiday destination

Let us take Turkey as an example of a destination which increased in popularity in the 1980s.

♦ At the beginning of the decade, Turkey was the kind of destination which appealed to an upmarket type of client, who possibly liked sailing or visiting unusual places but almost certainly did not like to go away with a large crowd of noisy and conspicuous British holidaymakers.

♦ Those clients were probably prepared to pay a little more than the average for their holiday, because they may have felt they were getting a real bargain when they finally reached Turkey, with its different standard of living.

♦ Then, in the mid 1980s, some of the bigger tour operators realised the potential of this new destination and started to market it in a big way, even dedicating specialist brochures to Turkey.

♦ By 1990, all the big tour operators included Turkey as a destination, the clients who 'discovered' it eight years previously had largely moved on to other interests and the basic price for a holiday was competitive with other Mediterranean destinations. Turkish holiday resorts had developed at a fantastic rate in response to the new demand but already there were rumblings of discontent among those clients who arrived to find their hotel in the middle of a building site or the road to the hotel inaccessible.

A holiday destination can therefore be said to follow the product life cycle with its initial discovery, its popularity and, finally, signs of decline in popularity.

Once this stage of decline is reached with any product, a decision has to be taken, whether or not to launch a new marketing initiative to revitalise the product. In Diagram 11.4 this decision point is marked by the letter Y. If the decision is taken to extend its life, then the strategy adopted will be concerned with at least one of the four Ps in the marketing mix. The changes must be made in

♦ the Product,

♦ the Place,

♦ the Price or

♦ the Promotion.

The product, or holiday itself, may have to be radically changed in terms of the accommodation and the services offered. The place may have to be changed in terms of the destination itself and the departure or return airport.

Changes in these areas have been quite controversial at times because they have involved **consolidation**. This is when clients have been asked to take holidays in places other than those originally chosen, or even depart from points other than those they originally booked. Such consolidation is sometimes done to ensure a viable number of people using a flight or a hotel but, understandably, it is not popular with the public and it is not encouraged by ABTA.

Changes may be made in the pricing structure so that the cost could be reduced, and holidays sold off at a special rate as late availability. The change could also be in the means of promoting the holiday, with more emphasis placed on letting the public know about the advantages of the holiday.

Changes could of course be made in more than one sector of the marketing mix but the changes will most certainly affect at least one of these areas.

Market Segmentation

In considering Turkey as a destination, we saw that it appealed to different clients at each stage of its development. This is a very important consideration in any marketing strategy and it is known as market segmentation. If we take a segment of anything, such as a piece of cake, we only have a part of it. In the same way, market segmentation is concerned with that part of the general public who are likely to be interested in the product or holiday we have to offer.

It is difficult to be all things to all people and so most companies consider their potential customer and concentrate on satisfying their particular needs and wants. This may mean that the bigger companies produce different brochures to appeal to different clients. Market segmentation can be based on:

♦ demographic factors, such as age;
♦ geography;
♦ socio-economic groupings;
♦ behavioural patterns, such as life style and attitudes;
♦ volume of business.

Demographic Segmentation

Demographic segmentation according to age has become quite common in the travel industry, with brochures which appeal to a particular age group whether it be the 18–30 age group, or to the over 55 type of holiday offered by Saga. It would be a good idea, if you have not done so already, to use your time on work placement to list the brochures which are aimed at different age groups. It might also be interesting to see how the one resort, such as Benidorm in Spain, is presented in the different brochures according to the age of the potential customers.

Geographic Segmentation

Geographic segmentation of the market could be by considering the home base of the clients. Different brochures may be produced according to whether the clients are departing from London, Manchester or Glasgow. With geographic segmentation clients feel that they are getting a more personalised service, and the information printed in the brochure can be simplified.

Some tour operators specialise in one country or area of the world, whilst others produce specialist brochures according to countries. These practices are based on geographic segmentation.

Socio-economic Groupings

Most market researchers divide the general population into six categories according to their occupation and probable income. These are known as socio-economic groupings and they are listed in the box below.

> A   Higher managerial, administrative or professional.
> B   Middle managerial, administrative or professional.
> C1 Supervisory, clerical or junior managerial.
> C2 Skilled manual workers.
> D   Semi- and unskilled manual workers.
> E   Those on the lowest level of subsistence – state pensioners, unemployed, casual and lowest grade workers.

Groupings A, B, and C1 are regarded as middle class, and groupings C2 and D as working class. Group E is based purely on income and can, from the point of view of holidays, have a very mixed bag of interests and desires, but the common factor is that people in this group are unlikely to have sufficient money to be able to contemplate a holiday. While there cannot be a hard and fast rule about the holidays which people prefer,

Diagram 11.5 gives an indication of the type of holiday which might appeal to the various groupings.

Group	Class/type of job	Type of holiday
A	Upper middle class e.g. Managing Director	Independent, exclusive with quality, luxury and very possibly some special interest, such as gourmet meals or archaeology.
B	Middle class e.g. Bank Manager	Good grade hotel, more adventurous holidays, even 'trend-setting'. Possibly in a group, but not on a recognised package holiday.
C1	Lower middle class e.g. Office Supervisor	Tend to imitate the trend-setters even when they cannot really afford it; probably use a three star hotel on a package holiday possibly with some special interest, such as music or art.
C2	Skilled working class e.g. Electrician	Two or possibly three star hotel on a package holiday, possibly with some special interest based on hobbies.
D	Working class e.g. Labourer	Possibly one holiday abroad a year, probably a cheaper package to Spain.
E	State pensioners, unemployed, casual workers etc.	Probably little demand for holidays.

Diagram 11.5 Holiday preferences

Behavioural Market Segmentation

Behavioural or life style market segmentation is preferred by several of the larger tour operators who produce brochures which appeal to specialist segments of the market according to the way they live and spend their money, rather than on the amount of money they earn. Life style segmentation by a tour operator could mean producing brochures for holidays concerned with a specific activity such as golfing, skiing, touring areas of historical interest, etc.

Travel agents also use a life style segmentation of the market when they make a conscious decision to appeal to one particular type of client. The decision may be taken to concentrate on upmarket, long haul holidays and cruises which may result in fewer, but more lucrative bookings. Lunn Poly and many other travel agents concentrate on offering a good, fast service for the client who wants a package holiday at the cheapest price and with the least fuss.

In order to cater for their desired clients it may therefore be necessary for a travel agent to display the brochures of only a certain number of preferred tour operators, although it is usual to keep office copies of all brochures received.

Volume Segmentation

Volume segmentation means dividing the market according to the amount of past business done by the client.

Airlines in particular use volume segmentation when they offer discounts, or even free tickets, to clients who book over a certain number of miles of flying in a year. This can be a very good marketing tool as it encourages good clients to become loyal and make repeat bookings and so further increase business.

Whatever the speciality or segmentation adopted it means that:

♦ the marketing team can concentrate on appealing to the needs and wants of that specific group;

♦ the application of the service can be simpler;

♦ the service offered can be improved.

◇ *Activity 11.2* ◇

Collect together the current brochures for the following cruise lines. You may have already used these brochures for Activity 10.2 (page 144).

♦ Cunard's *QE2* programme

♦ Cunard's *Vistafjord* and *Sagafjord* programme

♦ P & O's *Canberra* programme

♦ P & O's *Princess* Voyages

♦ Royal Caribbean Cruises

♦ CTC Cruises

♦ Equity Cruises.

Go through the brochures and make a list of selling slogans from each brochure. For example:

'A world dedicated to the best'
or, *'Let the real world slip your mind'*
or, *'A priceless holiday you will never forget'*.

Examine the selling slogans and photographs in each brochure and comment on the image that is being offered and the clientele, or market, to whom you think each brochure is directed.

For instance, does the brochure emphasise elegance and sophistication? Or is the accent on entertainment and enjoyment? Or is the major consideration value for money?

You could take your study even further by comparing the approach in brochures of the same company, such as Cunard's *QE2* and *Vistafjord/Sagafjord* programmes, or P & O's *Canberra* and *Princess* voyages.

Market Research

A marketing team collects and analyses data to help management in their decisions, and to monitor the results of those decisions. Market research is usually carried out with regard to:

♦ the consumer or client;

♦ the product or holiday;

♦ distribution of brochures and information;

♦ the effectiveness of promotions and advertising.

The data may be collected by carrying out surveys or questionnaires, which is called primary research. Information may also be collected by examining data in the company's files, or in public records and this is referred to as secondary research.

Primary Research Methods

Experimental research using surveys and questionnaires can be undertaken by post, telephone, door-to-door questioning, and/or stopping people in the street.

Research done by post can be cheap and quick and helps to preserve anonimity of the respondents. However, the questionnaires must be short and concise if a good response is to be obtained. The researchers will be limited in the amount of knowledge of the attitudes and background of the respondents that they can collect.

Telephone contact can be on a more personal level and, whilst it is more expensive than postal research, it is still a lot cheaper than personal interviews. The questions asked must be carefully designed so that they do not require too much thought for a response. These types of surveys can be very successful but their popularity may decline as more companies use this method and the public come to regard them as nuisance calls.

Street interviews are regarded by some people as a nuisance and the sample of people questioned can be heavily influenced by the fact that some busy people may refuse to stop and take part in the survey.

A survey is used to determine the views of a large group by approaching a smaller group so, by definition, the sample of people used should be representative of the larger group. It is not our concern here to master calculations of the numbers for sample groups, but it should be noted that the larger the number of people interviewed the greater the accuracy of the predictions which can be made.

With regard to accuracy in surveys, there comes a point in the number interviewed when 90 or 95 per cent accuracy can be expected. After this point the number of interviewees has to be greatly increased to improve the accuracy of the response even a little. In fact, to increase the level of accuracy by only another 5 per cent, the number of people interviewed would have to be four times greater.

In most surveys, the cost of complete accuracy cannot be justified, and most companies settle for 95 per cent accuracy.

The design of the questionnaire can greatly affect the accuracy of the responses received. The following should be avoided wherever possible:

♦ questions involving opinions, which are more difficult to analyse than those involving facts;

♦ complicated questions, which may be affected by the understanding, or lack of it, of those who are being interviewed;

♦ controversial or personal questions, which may receive a negative response because people are simply unwilling to answer them;

♦ questions relating to the future because they depend very much on the likelihood of the respondents changing their minds, or circumstances surrounding the decision being changed for them;

♦ questions involving reasons for decisions because the answers may not be received from the appropriate persons. For example the decision as to which travel agent is used may depend on where the mother of a family does her weekly shopping or which travel agency is near to the father's workplace. In this case it might really be irrelevant to ask the teenage son which travel agency he uses and why.

Structured questionnaires try to eliminate some of these inaccuracies by listing a rigid set of questions to which there are a set number of answers. This type of questionnaire is used in postal surveys as it is least open to misinterpretation and misunderstanding. However, it is very often unsuitable for complex situations.

Semi-structured questionnaires give a set of questions, together with instructions for the interviewer to cope with a range of response patterns. This leads to more flexibility for the responses and can be combined with open-ended or multi-choice questions to cover topics in greater depth.

Unstructured questionnaires are really just notes which the interviewer makes as a topic is investigated. They are open to far more inaccuracy on the part of both the interviewer and the respondent. Consequently, the data or information obtained is far more difficult to analyse. This type of questionnaire can, however, be very useful for a pilot survey to establish the correct procedure and layout for the actual research.

A modern popular alternative to the questionnaire is the consumer panel, where a group of customers might be asked to meet and chat, with direction, about the holidays they have booked, which ones they have enjoyed and which they have disliked. The results of the discussion can then be analysed.

Secondary Research Methods

The object of market research is to identify the total demand for the company's product in the market and then to highlight the potential customers. The examination of the company's files and public records can help to achieve a more complete picture of the situation.

A travel agent's files will usually include a record of their bookings. These records are kept according to the:

♦ date when bookings are made;

♦ tour operator or company with whom they are made;

♦ number of clients;

♦ number of children in the party;

♦ length of the holiday;

♦ departure point;

♦ type of accommodation.

Such a record book can be very useful the following year in deciding key dates for a promotional evening or when to place an advertisement in the local paper. These records could also help the travel agent to decide which brochures should be given full display and coverage in the agency. The effectiveness of these records are shown by the fact that they are common practice in most agencies, including the large multiples.

Multiple travel agencies usually have to report information about the timings and frequency of bookings to their Head Office where the function of market research is carried out on a national basis.

Tour operators keep records of the sales made by travel agencies and it is common practice for agents to receive their quota of brochures from the larger companies in direct proportion to the number of bookings made in the previous year.

Public records can be used to increase the company's awareness of any demographic or social changes likely to influence the success of the product. For example, when interest rates are high or unemployment is high, holidays may be regarded as a luxury in the family budget and this could adversely affect sales of holidays.

In all of these activities there is an element of forecasting and for this the team can use historical projections where they build on past trends in the travel industry.

◊ *Activity 11.3* ◊

If you are on a college course, with the help of your tutor, design and carry out a suitable survey. Possible topics for a survey are listed below.

1 In a local resort or tourist attraction, survey the reasons for people visiting; how far they have come; the type of accommodation they are using; and whether or not they would return to the area again.

2 Co-operate with a local travel agency to establish the opinions of people in your town with respect to that agency.

3 If your town or area has more than ten travel agencies, survey the opinions of local people with regard to which agency they use; the reasons for using/not using each agency; opinions with regard to brochures carried, service given and the attitude of the staff.

4 Survey holiday patterns over the past year in your town or college. Have people gone abroad or stayed in Britain; how and where did they book their holiday; which tour operators are the most popular; what kind of accommodation was used; what kind of transport; what were the likes and dislikes; were there any serious complaints?

The list of ideas for surveys is really endless but, as you prepare your survey, try to be scientific in your selection of the sample used, the type of questionnaire and the means of analysing the results.

Significant results from any of these surveys could be written up in the form of an interesting article for your local newspaper.

10 STEPS TO GOOD MARKETING SKILLS IN TRAVEL

1 Be clear about the problem.

2 Decide what information you need in terms of the four Ps of the marketing mix.

3 Try to identify the type of client to which you will appeal.

4 If necessary, design a research project.

5 Construct questionnaires carefully.

6 Carry out the research scientifically.

7 Analyse the data obtained.

8 Prepare a report and recommendations.

9 Choose an appropriate means of promotion bearing in mind AIDA.

10 Reap the success of your efforts and monitor your progress.

◊ *Revision Questions* ◊

1 Name three methods which a travel agent could use for advertising.

2 With regard to market segmentation, name five different types of brochures which are produced by tour operators.

3 Give two reasons for this practice of producing different brochures as in Question 2.

4 State three marketing activities of an English Regional Tourist Board.

5 If a resort or holiday destination were declining in popularity, give three marketing strategies which might be employed to revitalise interest amongst potential clients.

6 Very often, travel agents keep records of bookings to help with their marketing in the following year. Suggest two headings under which you could collect such information.

7 Market research information can be collected from primary or secondary sources. Give one example of each type.

8 Suggest three ways in which an independent travel agent could use a logo to help market their business.

9 Suggest three ways in which a large multiple travel agency chain could use their corporate image in marketing.

10 Suggest two ways in which a travel agent might encourage more bookings through a promotional evening.

12 *Retail Travel Practices*

By the end of this chapter you should have increased your:

♦ **knowledge of sources of income for a travel agent, levels of commission and the bonds and licences required by a new agency;**

♦ **skills in exercising prudence when granting credit, controlling costs in a travel agency and noting essential information to process a booking.**

Income

Without income and profit a travel agent will not stay in business. The main sources of income for a travel agent are:

♦ commission from principals,

♦ service charges and

♦ interest on any money held in the possession of the travel agent.

Commission is payment made to the travel agent by a principal such as a tour operator, airline or ferry company. The payment received is a percentage of the value of the booking made by the travel agent. Commission earned from principals on bookings varies between only 1 per cent on travellers cheques, to 37 per cent, or more, on insurance. The average package holiday tour operator gives a travel agent 10 per cent commission, but for selling scheduled international airline tickets the travel agent can earn 9 per cent, with only $7\frac{1}{2}$ per cent on domestic tickets, and about 9 per cent for car ferry bookings.

With a massive 37 per cent commission on insurance, it is understandable that most travel agents try to sell their own rather than the tour operator's insurance. The travel agent tries to predict the expected business for a particular principal and then calculates the expected commission, or income, before deciding which brochures to stock.

> If a package holiday costs £350 per person and there are four persons travelling, then the total value of the booking is £1400. A commission of 10 per cent would yield £140 in earnings.
>
> If however the booking were for two people taking a cruise at a cost of £3500 each, the total value of the booking is £7000 and the commission earned at 10 per cent would be £700.

The effort of making the booking would probably be the same in each case but the financial return is very different.

Coach operators usually give 10 per cent commission and, with an average price of a ticket taken at £10, a booking for four would yield a £4 commission. British Rail only give 7 per cent commission but the prices of average train journeys are greater than for coach trips, thus increasing the total commission paid. However, balance this with the greater time which could be spent in recommending a rail route and not all travel agents choose to become British Rail agents.

Incentive commission is offered by British Rail, along with some tour operators and car hire companies. This means that the travel agent with higher turnover, or business, for that principal receives a higher rate of commission. Some tour operators also extend credit facilities to travel agents who do regular business with them. In some cases a travel agent might be appointed as the 'sole agency' for a principal in a particular locality. If these travel agents accept bookings from other travel agents in the area then they receive **overrider commission** which allows them to pay standard commission to the other travel agents.

Service charges may be made by a travel agent just as they can be made in any retail outlet. Normally they are not a great source of income but are simply a means of recouping money on a transaction which might other-wise cost the travel agent some of their commission. A service charge may be made on a theatre booking to cover the cost of the telephone call to the booking office of the theatre. A service charge may also be made if the travel agent applies for a visa on behalf of a client. For business travellers there may be service charges in connection with the delivery of tickets and the revalidation or reissue of tickets.

In nearly all cases service charges are made simply to cover the costs of telephone calls, telexes or postage and in no way can they be regarded as a main source of income.

Interest on money held by the travel agent can be a major source of income. Such money held by a travel agent is sometimes referred to as **pipeline money** because it has been received from the client but has not as yet been passed on to the principal.

Monies to principals are normally sent at the end of each month. Forms, or returns, have to be filled out for each principal, showing the business done during the previous month and the amount of money taken in deposits and final payments.

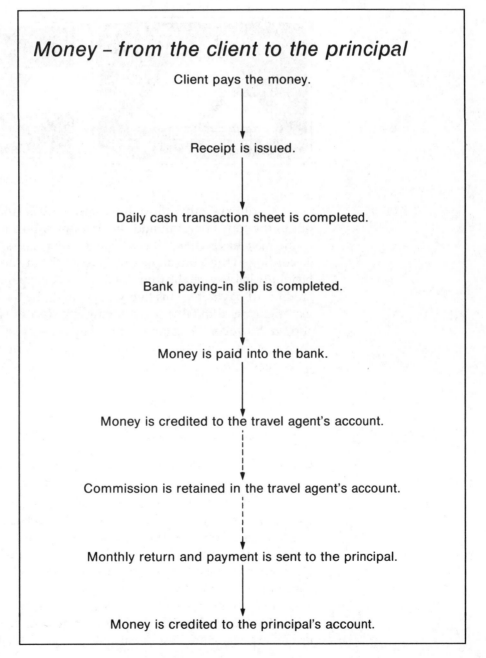

Money – from the client to the principal

Client pays the money.

↓

Receipt is issued.

↓

Daily cash transaction sheet is completed.

↓

Bank paying-in slip is completed.

↓

Money is paid into the bank.

↓

Money is credited to the travel agent's account.

↓

Commission is retained in the travel agent's account.

↓

Monthly return and payment is sent to the principal.

↓

Money is credited to the principal's account.

Diagram 12.1

Diagram 12.1 (page 165) shows the route taken by money paid in to a travel agent by a client. The dotted line between the money going into the travel agent's account and the money being paid into the principal's account indicates that this time is variable depending on the time of the month when the money was received.

Money which has been paid by a client, before a booking is confirmed, is held in trust for that client. This means that, should the principal be declared insolvent, the money will be returned to the client. If, however, a booking has been confirmed, then the travel agent holds the money in trust for the principal, and should the latter's business fold, the client would have to make a claim as a creditor just as if the money had already been paid over to the principal.

If a client pays either the deposit or the full balance by credit card, made out to the tour operator, and the amount comes to more than £100, the client may have an additional means of redress, if the business folds. According to the Consumer Credit Act 1974 the credit card company will be jointly liable with the tour operator or principal which has accepted the credit card payment. This knowledge might be useful to the client who is experiencing difficulty in receiving satisfaction about a complaint. It should, however, be remembered that the act applies only to *credit* cards such as Access and Visa, and not to *charge* cards such as American Express or Diners Club.

Granting Credit

Some travel agencies have a **business house** where they deal, very often by telephone, with local firms. Such businesses may deal exclusively with a travel agent, expecting them to process tickets, car hire and other services, sometimes at very short notice. Where a travel agent has a large business house interest the question of granting credit may arise.

Granting credit can have its advantages because it ensures maximum business from a particular company and it binds that company with a firm commitment to the travel agent.

On the other hand, it could be risky because granting credit reduces the flow of actual cash. If the business wants a special discount, this could erode any real commission earned.

However, if on balance the travel agent decides that it would be worthwhile to offer credit to businesses then care must be taken on a number of points.

♦ The business in question should be well-known to the travel agent.

♦ The business should have already completed a number of cash transactions with the agent, before credit is granted.

♦ A financial statement on a business for the purpose of credit worthiness can be obtained. The travel agent's own bank manager would probably be able to help in recommending a consultant for this purpose.

♦ As principals normally offer only one month's credit to the travel agent, it is unwise for the travel agent to offer more than a month's credit to other businesses.

♦ Discreet enquiries can always be made with the business' bankers, although the message received may have to be decoded because a bank is unlikely to discredit a client outright. A bank which has doubts about a client might use phrases such as 'we have insufficient knowledge about this client', rather than an enthusiastic 'we have no hesitation in recommending this client for credit'. As in all references, the travel agent has to read between the lines to imagine what has not been said about the client.

◊ *Activity 12.1* ◊

While on work placement research the current levels of commission from the following principals:

a) British Rail,
b) A large tour operator,
c) A smaller tour operator,
d) A car-carrying ferry company,
e) A local car hire firm,
f) An international car hire firm,
g) A coach company,
h) An insurance company,
i) A cruise line.

Ask the travel agent at your work placement about any incentive or overrider commission offered by the companies.

Bonds and Licences

A **bond** is a type of insurance taken out by a travel company, possibly with a bank, so that, if the company ceases trading, costs can be covered for repatriating, or bringing home, clients or compensating clients for the loss of a holiday or flight.

If the company ceases trading, secured creditors, such as banks and the Inland Revenue, have first claim on any money which can be paid out. Legally the client would be an unsecured creditor with no specific claim against the assets of the company. In other words, without a bond to pay them out, the client would probably not receive any compensation for a lost holiday or uncompleted travel arrangement.

In Chapter Three we saw that British tour operators may be required to take out an ATOL licence and lodge a bond with the Civil Aviation Authority. All ABTA travel agents and tour operators are obliged to lodge a bond with ABTA. Some of the larger multiple travel agents, such as American Express, Lunn Poly and W H Smith cover all bookings with their own bonding scheme in addition to the ABTA bond.

Membership of ABTA is not easily given because a new travel agent must be actively trading successfully before such membership is granted. This is not easy when you consider the ABTA rule commonly referred to as **stabiliser**, which was defined in Chapter Three (see page 35). 'Stabiliser' means in effect that non-ABTA travel agents cannot sell the more popular package holidays.

However, there is still a wide range of domestic holidays and travel services which potential ABTA travel agents can offer, such as:

♦ rail travel,

♦ coach travel,

♦ hotel bookings,

♦ holiday camps and

♦ car ferry services.

Once trading has been established, application can be made to ABTA for membership and a range of information will be requested, including:

♦ photographs of the shop's interior and exterior;

♦ details of the staff qualifications;

♦ evidence of past trading;

♦ the business accounts;

♦ a non-refundable registration fee.

An ABTA application takes approximately three months to process and during this time the agency will receive an unannounced visit from a representative of ABTA. If successful, the new travel agent will:

♦ be given an ABTA licence number which should be used for identification in all publications, advertisements and business with other ABTA members;

♦ have to lodge a bond with ABTA to cover costs should the company fold;

♦ pay an annual subscription based on the company's turnover, in order to retain membership of ABTA.

Having obtained an ABTA licence, the travel agent can then apply to principals, such as tour operators and airlines for a licence to hold stocks of brochures, tickets and point of sale material. It is usual for principals to draw up an agreement with travel agents through which the principal has details of the company and their practices. The travel agent knows the commission to be earned, as well as how and when to make payments.

ABTA issues codes of conduct for both tour operators and travel agents. The Tour Operators' Code of Conduct details:

♦ minimum standards for brochures;

♦ guidelines for booking conditions;

♦ correct procedure in the event of alterations or overbooking;

♦ cancellation procedures;

♦ complaints procedures;

♦ good practice with regard to advertising.

A tour operator's brochure should not demand that clients make a complaint known within an unreasonable period of time, such as a week after returning from holiday. According to the Code, the period for accepting complaints should be more than 28 days, giving clients time to consider their situation.

Tour operators may not cancel holidays for reasons other than those beyond their control, such as earthquakes, hurricanes or a state of war. In other circumstances, clients should be offered reasonable alternatives or a full refund which must be sent to the agent within ten clear days or direct to the client within 14 clear days.

The Travel Agents' Code of Conduct demands a high standard of ABTA travel agents who are required to:

♦ make every effort to give accurate and impartial information to their clients so that they can buy holidays or travel arrangements which are compatible with their individual requirements;

♦ offer help to the client as regards filling out the booking form, taking out suitable insurance cover, as well as offering advice about passports, visas, health requirements and foreign currency;

♦ act as an intermediary if a dispute arises and try to reach a friendly solution in the quickest possible time.

Misleading material should not appear in any advertisement or publication of an ABTA member and each member's ABTA number should be clearly shown. In this way the public can always refer to the tour operator's or travel agent's official ABTA number and name if they wish to contact ABTA about a complaint.

Keeping Records

One of the most important documents in a travel agency is the form on which initial enquiries are noted. This is referred to under various names but we shall call it an **option form**. Whether the client first makes a telephone call or a personal visit, it is most important that all relevant details are taken, so that the booking can be made correctly if the client chooses a holiday. These details are also needed so that the potential client can be contacted again, if they want time to make up their mind, or they want the agent to make more enquiries.

An option form can help, not only in recording this information, but also in reminding the travel agent to ask appropriate questions. The essential information needed includes the:

♦ client's name, address and telephone number,

♦ date of travel,

♦ departure point,

- ♦ destination required,
- ♦ number of nights for a holiday,
- ♦ chosen hotel or apartment,
- ♦ means of transport,
- ♦ preferred brochure or travel company,
- ♦ names of any other members of the party and
- ♦ ages of any children who will be travelling.

Once the client's details are noted an enquiry can be made with a principal and, if the holiday is available and is not a late booking, the travel agent can take out an **option**.

> An option means that the booking is accepted by the principal and is held in the client's name for a stated period of time. This time is usually 24 hours, which is long enough for the client to pay the required deposit. If the booking is not confirmed within that period of time, the holiday arrangements are placed on sale again.

The **option reference** and **expiry date**, by which the booking must be confirmed, should be carefully noted in the appropriate space on the option form. Many option forms also include space for a costing and any special requests from the client. In some agencies separate option forms are designed for package holiday and travel arrangements-only bookings.

◇ *Activity 12.2* ◇

While on work placement, critically examine the form used in the travel agency for recording initial enquiries. Some agencies have a simple form with boxes for the required information. Others have sophisticated pads designed around the name of the company which look good, but do not necessarily help the agent to record the required information.

Design your own option form, making sure you include spaces or boxes for all the essential information listed above.

Once you have designed the option form, role-play a holiday booking with a friend or colleague. You are aiming to test the usefulness of the form as a prompt to help you ask appropriate questions and record all necessary information.

Receipts

Once a booking has been confirmed and a deposit paid by the client, a **receipt** has to be issued. Receipts should be issued for all money received, including cash, cheques and credit card transactions.

For security, receipts should have serial numbers and each one must be accounted for. If a mistake is made on a receipt it should not be thrown away, but the receipt can be made void with a line right through it. The

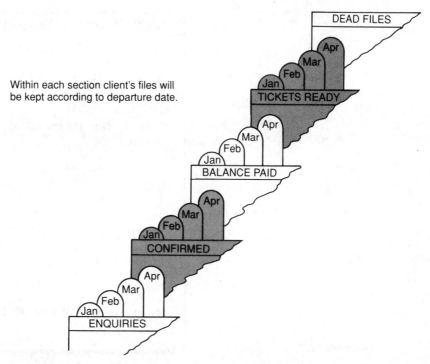

Within each section client's files will be kept according to departure date.

Diagram 12.2

information on the receipt should include the amount, the client's name and address and the date of the transaction. It should also include the name of the principal, the travel agent's name and ABTA and VAT numbers. It is usual to have at least three copies of the receipt. One is for the client, one is for the file and the third is for the travel agency's accounting system.

Filing Systems

A copy of this receipt, together with the option form and a copy of the brochure, if it is an unusual one, will form the start of a client file. Travel agencies may use either a manual or a computerised filing system for these client files.

In a manual filing system the file can be kept alphabetically under the surname of the client, or alternatively under the departure date of the booking. Filing by departure date is used so that it is easy to keep track of bookings. Full payment has to be sent to principals eight weeks before departure. Tickets should have arrived from principals two weeks before departure. A further refinement to filing by departure date is when the client's file is moved into different sections or drawers according to the current status of the booking.

As shown in Diagram 12.2, sections for such a filing system could be

♦ initial enquiries,

♦ confirmed bookings,

♦ bookings on which the balance has been paid, and

♦ bookings for which tickets have been received.

Once the client has taken a holiday, the client file is kept in a separate area, sometimes called a dead file, for a period of time of up to two years just in case there should be any problem or claim made at a later date.

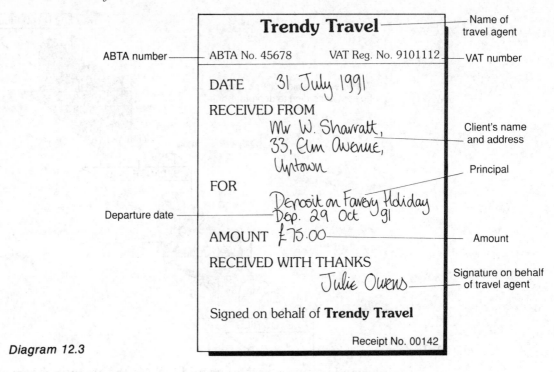

Trendy Travel ——— Name of
                              travel agent

ABTA number ——— ABTA No. 45678   VAT Reg. No. 9101112 ——— VAT number

DATE   31 July 1991

RECEIVED FROM

Mr W. Sharratt,   Client's name
33, Elm Avenue,   and address
Uptown

FOR   Principal

Departure date ——— Deposit on Fawery Holiday
                    Dep. 29 Oct '91

AMOUNT £75.00 ——— Amount

RECEIVED WITH THANKS

          Julie Owens ——— Signature on behalf
                           of travel agent

Signed on behalf of **Trendy Travel**

Receipt No. 00142

Diagram 12.3

With a computerised database, it is easier to access information
according to whatever aspect may be desired. The information is entered
into the database just as it might be on a manual filing system. However,
once the data is stored it is then possible to retrieve the information in
different ways.

A database could be ordered by departure date, and then reordered
alphabetically in a matter of seconds. The same file of information could be
used to select those bookings which had been made using a particular
airport, or even a particular hotel. This could be very useful if clients have
to be informed of any problems.

Diagram 12.4
Computer printout
showing clients'
holidays with July
departures, arranged by
departure date

Dep Date	Dep Airport	Destination	Hotel	Nights	Client
3 July	MAN	PMI	AZUL	7	WARNER
5 July	LHR	PMI	GRANADA	14	ASCOT
6 July	MAN	PMI	ALHAMBRA	14	CRAVEN
8 July	LGW	PMI	GRANADA	14	MOOR
10 July	MAN	PMI	AZUL	7	DAVIES
11 July	LHR	PMI	GRANADA	14	EDEN
15 July	MAN	PMI	ALHAMBRA	7	WALKER
18 July	NCL	PMI	AZUL	14	WILLIAMS
19 July	LGW	PMI	AZUL	7	HARRISON
21 July	MAN	PMI	GRANADA	14	BRIDGE
25 July	MAN	PMI	AZUL	7	PIMLOTT
27 July	LHR	PMI	ALHAMBRA	14	WRIGHT
30 July	LGW	PMI	GRANADA	7	COPE

Dep Date	Dep Airport	Destination	Hotel	Nights	Client
5 Jul	LHR	PMI	GRANADA	14	ASCOT
21 Jul	MAN	PMI	GRANADA	14	BRIDGE
30 Jul	LGW	PMI	GRANADA	7	COPE
6 Jul	MAN	PMI	ALHAMBRA	14	CRAVEN
10 Jul	MAN	PMI	AZUL	7	DAVIES
11 Jul	LHR	PMI	GRANADA	14	EDEN
19 Jul	LGW	PMI	AZUL	7	HARRISON
8 Jul	LGW	PMI	GRANADA	14	MOOR
25 Jul	MAN	PMI	AZUL	7	PIMLOTT
15 Jul	MAN	PMI	ALHAMBRA	7	WALKER
3 Jul	MAN	PMI	AZUL	7	WARNER
18 Jul	NCL	PMI	AZUL	14	WILLIAMS
27 Jul	LHR	PMI	ALHAMBRA	14	WRIGHT

Diagram 12.5 Computer printout showing clients' holidays with July departures arranged alphabetically by name

Dep Date	Dep Airport	Destination	Hotel	Nights	Client
3 July	MAN	PMI	AZUL	7	WARNER
6 July	MAN	PMI	ALHAMBRA	14	CRAVEN
10 July	MAN	PMI	AZUL	7	DAVIES
15 July	MAN	PMI	ALHAMBRA	7	WALKER
21 July	MAN	PMI	GRANADA	14	BRIDGE
25 July	MAN	PMI	AZUL	7	PIMLOTT

Diagram 12.6 Computer printout showing clients' departing from Manchester Airport in July, arranged by departure date

Dep Date	Dep Airport	Destination	Hotel	Nights	Client
10 Jul	MAN	PMI	AZUL	7	DAVIES
19 Jul	LGW	PMI	AZUL	7	HARRISON
25 Jul	MAN	PMI	AZUL	7	PIMLOTT
3 Jul	MAN	PMI	AZUL	7	WARNER
18 Jul	NCL	PMI	AZUL	14	WILLIAMS

Diagram 12.7 Computer printout showing clients who are staying at the Hotel Azul in July, arranged alphabetically by client's name

If the bookings requiring final payment need to be extracted, this could be done quickly through the computer, rather than having to physically move files from one drawer of a filing cabinet to another. The computer could be instructed to print out only the bookings needing final payment.

The larger multiple travel agencies have installed their own in-house systems. With the cost of powerful portable computers and their software coming down all the time, these sophisticated filing systems are now within reach of most travel agents. The Data Protection Act 1984 sets standards which must be observed where a computerised filing system is in use.

In larger organisations there may be an accounts department but, even in the smallest travel agency, there will be a means of keeping track of daily transactions. This can take the form of daily cash **reconciliation sheets**.

Diagram 12.8 shows an example of such a sheet. The serial numbers of receipts issued during the day are recorded along with the total amount of money taken. Any refunds issued are taken from this amount and a net figure is shown on the left hand side of the form. A record is also kept of any petty cash spent during the day and these items will be examined more closely when we consider controlling costs in an agency. Finally, the amount to be banked for the day is summarised in the bottom right hand corner. The procedure for banking is quite simple using the paying-in slips provided by the banks.

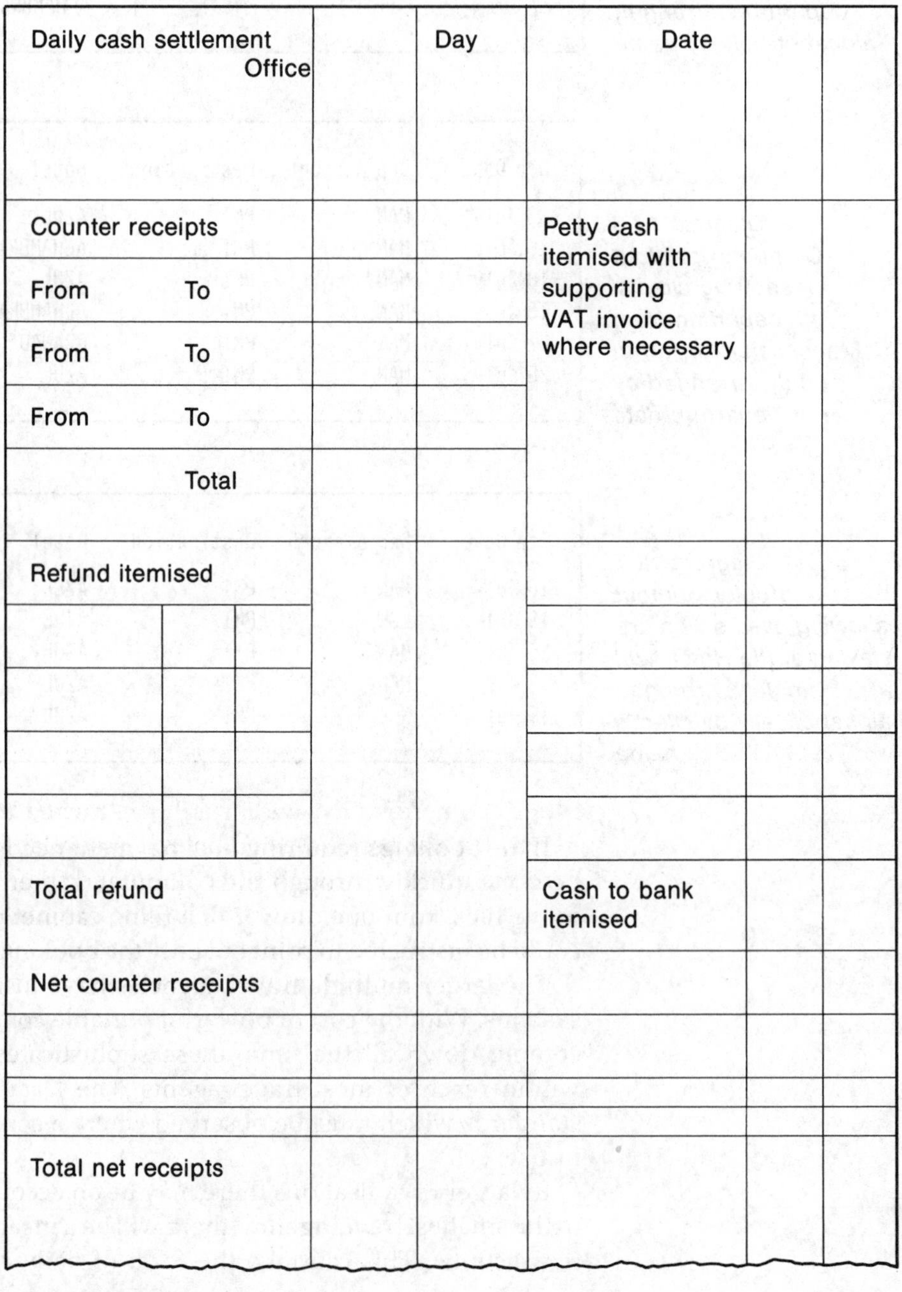

Daily cash settlement Office		Day	Date		
Counter receipts			Petty cash itemised with supporting VAT invoice where necessary		
From To					
From To					
From To					
Total					
Refund itemised					
Total refund			Cash to bank itemised		
Net counter receipts					
Total net receipts					

Diagram 12.8 Daily cash reconciliation sheet

Records of bookings have traditionally been kept in ledgers according to the principals involved. This is done to help the travel agent with marketing and sales plans in the following year. Such records will normally include information about the

♦ date the booking was made,

♦ the lead passenger name,

♦ the number of passengers,

♦ the departure date, and

♦ the destination.

All of this information will be entered under the appropriate principal's name. In this way it is easy to total the number and type of bookings made with a particular principal, as well as the time of year when most bookings were made. In the following year, this information may help the travel agent to decide the best month in which to launch a promotion with a particular principal.

Computerised systems make such a filing system easier because the information can be extracted from the main database if a selection is made under the name of the principal. In setting up a computerised travel agency database, careful consideration must be given from the beginning to the type of information which the agent may wish to extract from the system.

A brochure file contains copies of all brochures which are received in an agency. Whenever new brochures are stamped and displayed on the rack, the travel agent should always check that a file copy has been kept for reference. The brochure file copies are usually filed alphabetically, with subdivisions for summer and winter stock.

Tourist information files can also be kept alphabetically according to the country or resort. In this way, information can be accessed easily and quickly and the time taken to file the information is more than compensated for by the speed at which a client's request can be answered.

Controlling Costs

If the income detailed earlier is to be turned into profits for the travel agency, it must not be wasted on non-essential spending. In any business there are running costs to be covered and these include the lighting and heating bills for the premises, business rates, rent or mortgage repayments and staff salaries. Some of these costs are fixed but others can be controlled by the agency so that money and resources are not wasted.

Fixed costs must be paid if the business is to continue and these include the:

♦ rates;

♦ rent or mortgage for the property;

♦ essential repairs and improvements;

♦ staff salaries;

♦ insurance;

♦ standing or minimum charges for electricity, telephone and water charges.

However, **controllable costs** mean that:

♦ lighting and heating could be used to excess or could be kept to an adequate level;

♦ telephone calls could be made without thought of the cost, or the time and number of calls could be controlled;

♦ stationery items such as pens, pencils and paper could also be wasted, or used sparingly and in a controlled manner.

◇ *Activity 12.3* ◇

Generally speaking, the areas over which the travel agent has control with regard to cost are stationery, postage and telephone charges, cleaning, lighting, heating and petty cash spending.

While you are on your work placement discuss with the manager and staff the agency's policy with regard to savings on these items.

1 Stationery

♦ Does the agency have pre-printed stationery?

♦ Are scrap pads supplied for doodling or do staff waste pre-printed stationery?

♦ How and when are smaller items such as envelopes, pens, pencils ordered?

2 Postage

♦ Does the agency have a policy as regards which letters get a first class and which get a second class stamp?

3 Telephone charges

♦ Before you go on placement find out the different times of the day when telephone charges vary.

♦ Does the agency have a policy with regard to when calls may be made?

♦ What is the view of the manager on staff using the telephone for their personal calls?

♦ What is the view of the manager on the staff receiving calls during working hours?

♦ Do staff make a habit of having all essential information ready when they are about to make a call?

♦ Is there a list of useful freephone numbers (starting with the digits 0800)?

4 Cleaning

♦ Who does the cleaning?

♦ Is the agency kept in a general state of tidiness?

♦ Are the window displays designed so that they are accessible and easy to keep clean?

♦ Are used cups and mugs left lying around?

5 Lighting and heating

♦ Is there an area where the staff can be warm and comfortable during breaks?

♦ Is the agency warm and inviting?

♦ Is it well lit?

♦ Are lights left on in the evening or at night?

♦ Is there a policy with regard to lights being left on during the day?

6 Petty cash

♦ List the items bought with petty cash during an average week.

♦ What system does the agency use for keeping track of what is spent on petty cash?

♦ How much float is kept for petty cash?

♦ Is the petty cash float topped up each night?

◇ *Revision Questions* ◇

1 In a travel agency there are three possible sources of income – commission, interest and service charges. For each of the following transactions state which one of these would apply:
  a) arranging a visa,
  b) selling a package holiday,
  c) selling insurance,
  d) investing company funds,
  e) revalidating an airline ticket.

2 Name three fixed overhead costs in a travel agency.

3 Name three controllable costs in a travel agency.

4 State the standard commission which could be earned by a travel agent for each type of business below:
  a) British Rail ticket from Liverpool to Leeds,
  b) British Airways flight from London to Glasgow,
  c) travellers cheques issued from own office stock,
  d) car ferry from Dover to Calais,
  e) a fly/cruise to the Caribbean.

5 How many weeks before departure do most tour operators require a client to pay the balance?

6 Briefly describe one way in which a travel agent might keep track of important deadlines in a manual filing system.

7 In a business house situation, name two considerations which a travel agent would have to take into account before offering credit to a client.

8 Suggest a way in which a travel agent might be able to receive increased commission from a principal.

9 Name three requirements which would have to be fulfilled before ABTA membership could be granted to a travel agent.

10 What do you understand by the term 'pipeline money'?

13 *Selling Skills in a Travel Agency*

By the end of this chapter you should have increased your:

♦ knowledge of the steps in making a sale and the use of colour and lines in window display;

♦ skills with open and closed questions, benefit statements and dealing with difficult clients.

Steps in Making a Sale

What Attracts Clients to a Travel Agency?

The client must first be enticed into entering or telephoning the travel agent with an initial enquiry if they are eventually to make a firm booking. The initial attraction can be stimulated by:

♦ advertisements of the travel agent,

♦ advertisements of the principal,

♦ the travel agent's window display,

♦ the array of late availability cards to be found on the windows or doors of most agencies,

♦ the very arrangement of brochures on the racks within the agency.

Once the client has approached the travel agent, the welcome they receive is very important. It should be friendly and inviting without being too familiar, and it should stimulate further interest or action.

Some of the larger multiple travel agents put such emphasis on the importance of the welcome given to clients that their staff are trained to give a standard greeting to everyone entering or telephoning the agency.

The potential client may be very certain of the booking they require, but equally they may have only a vague idea of wanting a holiday but not where they would like to go. It is at this stage that professional selling skills will have scope as the travel agent tries to establish the basic reasons for that person wishing to take a holiday, and then identifies the real needs. The potential client may want:

♦ a quiet break,

♦ a week in the outdoors,

♦ to learn a new sport,

♦ a pilgrimage to a well-known shrine,

♦ a lively week and as much drinking as possible.

Without establishing these very different needs, the travel agent cannot hope to recommend a suitable arrangement and sell a holiday.

The next step is to offer the client a suitable holiday. This will most probably involve the skilful use of brochures and Viewdata systems to display the holiday's benefits for that particular client. The holiday should be appropriate to the needs that have already been identified, but if there is still some doubt it can be useful to recommend an expensive rather than a cheaper holiday. This will flatter the client and is almost bound to stimulate a reaction of either pleasure, or regret that it is out of the question.

Further investigation could then establish the actual needs more clearly. Any objections raised by the client can be used to clarify their real needs if the travel agent is sufficiently alert and sensitive.

Finally, the sale must be closed and this should be done in such a way that the client, impressed with the travel agent's efficiency and care, will want to return to that particular agency for future bookings.

The follow-up to the sale continues right through to the point where the client receives the correct tickets for the journey. Picture postcards displayed in some agencies testify to the many satisfied clients who remember their travel agent while on holiday.

Selling is in fact all about helping someone to reach a decision and we will now look in more detail at each of the stages in making a sale.

Attracting the Interest of the Client

Advertising

Advertising has two main aims:

♦ the obvious one of increasing sales, and

♦ the on-going aim of building up the reputation of the company with the public.

Travel agents can do their own advertising in newspapers and at local events. Sometimes they can share the costs with a principal, if they are doing sufficient business. Principals themselves have nationwide advertising campaigns, especially at the launch of a new brochure.

Travel agents should try to build on the impact of principals' advertisements. For example, a rearrangement of a brochure display to reinforce the television advertisements of the previous night could be very advantageous.

A good advertisement should give the potential client information about the product, as well as persuading them that the company has something different and better to offer. In the travel business many companies offer very similar products. A particular holiday could be to the same hotel, even using the same airport as that of a rival company. To attract the attention of their public, brochures emphasise advantages such as a guarantee of no surcharges, or a selected number of free child places. On transatlantic air crossings, the fare may be the same with different airlines, but the potential client could have to make a choice between a free teddy bear, free in-flight drinks or a free flight bag!

Free gifts can help to fulfil a third function of advertising, which is to maintain the image of the brochure or company, so that they stay in the mind of the public.

Late Availability Cards

Many travel agents put late availability cards in the window to attract clients.

> Late availability cards give details of holidays at reduced prices which usually have to be taken within the next few days.

The cards should be carefully checked each day to make certain that the holidays are still available. Not only can outdated cards be misleading to potential clients, who are disappointed if they enter the shop and find that the holiday has gone, but the travel agent could, in fact, be breaking the law.

> Trading Standards Officers are very aware of late availability cards and of their potential for offending against the Sale of Goods Act of 1979 or the Trades Description Act of 1968.

Window Displays

Window displays in travel agencies should attract potential clients by their overall impact and their colour. Some agencies prefer to seek professional help from companies which specialise in display techniques. The larger multiples often have a company directive for changing displays. However, in many agencies it is still a job which is done by the staff themselves.

The display should be arranged to produce definite lines if it is to achieve the greatest impact. Vertical lines give a dramatic appearance, whilst horizontal lines inspire tranquility. Curving lines are soft and gentle, but diagonal lines can have a startling effect.

Balance is important in a formal display, with an identical right and left side, to imply harmony. An informal display, which is not symmetrical, has potential to show contrasts.

An awareness of colour can help, especially if the display is to have a seasonal effect.

♦ *Red* is a strong, emotional and highly visible colour and is especially associated with Christmas.

♦ *Orange* is warm and inspires homely thoughts of autumn and harvest-time.

♦ *Yellow* is cheerful and sunny, implying sunshine, spring and new life.

♦ *Green* is a very relaxing colour with associations of calmness and freshness as well as the political use of it for all that is natural and good for the environment.

♦ *Blue* inspires thoughts of quiet and peace as well as water, air and great distances.

♦ *Brown* is a drab colour, which is not usually helpful in a display.

♦ *White* or *black* can be very useful as highlights for the other colours.

Brochure Display

The brochure display can project an image of the travel agent to the potential client, and thus influence their decision whether or not to make that initial enquiry. A cluttered brochure display which lacks order does not promise that the travel agent will deal very efficiently with the booking! A brochure which is out of stock cannot reach its sales potential, no matter how good the advertising campaign associated with it!

Brochures which are displayed to advantage can help the client to reach their decision about a holiday. Earlier, it was suggested that the display could be used to reinforce a national advertising campaign and, if this is to be done effectively, the travel agent should be aware of the importance of positioning brochures to have maximum impact (shelf planogram).

♦ Position the brochures attractively and make sure that they are well stocked.

♦ A brochure you wish to promote should be displayed at eye level and should be easily accessible.

♦ Special attention should be given to the brochures placed to the right of the ones you wish to promote. The eye moves naturally from left to right so the products to the right will receive more attention from the client than those on the left.

Some travel agents prefer to rack cards or display-copies of brochures so that the client has to ask for a brochure. In this way, it is hoped that the client will be committed more quickly to a selling situation. Most principals agree that it takes on average ten brochures to produce one firm booking.

The larger multiple travel agents have a Head Office policy on shelf layouts, preferred brochures, shelf strips and lighting, giving a common appearance to their shops throughout the country.

◊ *Activity 13.1* ◊

In your local area, visit about ten travel agencies and survey the following.

1 Look at the impact of the window display. Is there a definite use of colour? Is the display formal or informal? Is there a theme?

2 Observe the use of brochures for display purposes. They can be folded and stapled to achieve a number of effects. Discuss the effect with the travel agent and try to learn three different ways of folding and using brochures in displays.

3 Inside the agency, look at the way the brochures are displayed. Is there a limited number of brochures, or is there a great selection and variety of brochures on show? Is there any definite order to the racking? Are there labels on the shelves? Which brochures are placed at eye level?

Welcoming the Client

First impressions are always important but never more so than in a selling situation where the potential client has to decide in an instant whether or not they can trust the person who is trying to sell them a product. We all make subconscious judgements about each other based very largely on our past experiences. If the travel agent is conscious of the impression which is being made, it is possible through sensitivity and experience to increase the influence of certain desirable qualities such as a good appearance, a welcoming form of greeting and a pleasant, attentive attitude.

Appearance

General appearance is so important that many travel agencies provide a uniform for their staff. Whether or not there is a uniform, the travel agent should aim to be clean and smart in their dress, as well as in the way they walk or stand. The travel agent's physique and general health should be such that the long day in the agency does not impair their alertness or cause them to lounge or lean on the counters or desk.

A good appearance can inspire confidence in the potential client who will assume that they will be offered a courteous, efficient service. If the travel agent is untidy and the desk is in a mess, the potential client cannot be blamed for thinking that a person who cannot look after themselves is unlikely to be able to look after a booking with care and attention.

Greeting the Client

The first words of greeting are very important, but equally important is the tone in which they are spoken. When greeting a client it is best to avoid slang, colloquial language and swearing which would almost certainly give offence. The travel agent should not be over familiar because the client is expecting service, not friendship.

The question, 'Can I help you?' is not a very good way of greeting because it can immediately inspire a response of 'No thank you, just looking'. It is far better to be positive and ask where the person was thinking of going, or even, watching the brochures which take their interest, to start to talk about a particular place.

The overall impression given by the voice is affected by the volume, speed, pitch and tone of voice. The words 'I'll be with you in a moment', can be said in a number of ways.

♦ They can be used to imply that the client is a nuisance who is interfering with the travel agent's private thoughts or activity.

♦ They can be said with sincerity and mean that the client will have the agent's full attention in just a moment, when they are finished with another important task.

The voice can be affected by the feelings of a person, and if the travel agent is in a situation where they are nervous, or even angry, taking a few deep breaths can help to get the voice back under control.

Other qualities are more difficult to define but they are concerned with the travel agent's mental approach. The agent should:

♦ be attentive,

♦ listen to the client,

♦ be confident yet sensitive,

♦ use eye contact to inspire confidence, and

♦ have an outgoing friendly attitude.

> Sociability is the art of getting on with other people and the travel agent needs this quality. They should be outgoing, helpful and sincere without being either aggressive or too shy.

Character or maturity will put the finishing touches to a personality reflecting cheerfulness, honesty, consistency and a sense of responsibility.

A study of body language would help to reveal hidden clues to the attitude of the travel agent. A person who is untidy, who constantly fiddles and clicks a pen, who looks around the room in a distracted manner or sits at the desk eating and drinking will not inspire the confidence of a potential client.

The travel agent who tries to develop desirable qualities can only increase their sales potential.

Investigating the Client's Needs

Bearing in mind that most brochures are also available in other agencies, the travel agent's main sales tool is the conversation with the client. In the course of the conversation, the aim is to establish the client's needs as regards

♦ where,

♦ when,

♦ how, and

♦ why they wish to travel or go on holiday.

Once these needs have been identified, then the travel agent can actually sell a holiday or travel arrangement to suit the client.

Rapport, or a relationship and bond, should be established with the client. Rapport, while not meaning familiarity, will give an atmosphere of closeness, harmony and mutual understanding.

Within this atmosphere, the travel agent needs to ask questions which will inspire answers other than, 'Yes', or, 'No'. Closed questions, such as, 'Do you want to fly from Manchester?' can be changed to open questions such as 'From which airport would you like to fly?'. Open questions give more opportunity for the client to express a preference and will help the conversation to continue, so that more needs can be identified.

> The secret of formulating open questions is to use the questioning words of where, when, who, why, what, which and how.

Selling Skills in a Travel Agency

◇ *Activity 13.2* ◇

By using the questioning words of where, when, who, why, what, which or how, change the following closed questions to open questions. Try to use a different word to start each one.

1 Do you want to go in August?

2 Will there be just you and your husband travelling?

3 Do you want to go to Spain?

4 Do you want self-catering?

5 Do you want to be near a beach?

6 Is it for two weeks?

7 Do you want a room with a seaview and balcony?

8 Do you want a morning flight?

Telephone Enquiries

When a client is making enquiries by telephone, the conversation should be controlled by the travel agent so that the required information can be elicited. Option forms, which were discussed in detail in Chapter Twelve, can be a good prompt to remind the travel agent to ask all the appropriate questions when using the telephone.

The effective use of the voice is very important on the telephone especially when we realise that most of us only listen to about a third of what is said to us. When using the telephone the travel agent should make a conscious effort to:

♦ listen to the client,

♦ limit the information given over the telephone,

♦ summarise and check details at the end of the call.

When a client telephones an agent and relies on their judgement and professional skill to find an appropriate holiday or travel arrangement, the travel agent must take particular care.

> The travel agent could be held liable by a client if they could be shown to have used a tour operator or other principal whom they had reason to believe was unreliable in some way. It would certainly be no defence, in fact it would be confirmation of guilt, for a travel agent to admit that they thought a particular company was unreliable in its practices.

Presenting the Product to the Client ———————

Once the client's needs have been established, the travel agent must use knowledge, skill and experience to select and present a holiday or travel arrangement best suited to that client's needs. The rapport which has been established should be continued so that the presentation can be as personal as possible.

The presentation can be made more personal by generating enthusiasm and personalising statements so that a description of the features of a holiday are turned into a list of benefits for the client.

♦ The hotel may have a disco in the basement, but this can be personalised for a young person by saying that there is a disco on site so there is no need to be out late at night and go to the expense of taxis.

♦ Equally, for an older person, the travel agent might describe the basement disco, saying that it is out of hearing from the bedrooms and, while it provides entertainment for the young people at night, it is a great place during the day for bingo sessions and tea dances.

The key phrase to creating a benefit statement is 'which means that ...' After this phrase, the personal benefit to the client can be expressed. For example, 'The hotel has three restaurants,' could be expressed as, 'The hotel has three restaurants, which means that you can have a variety of meals and decor, all without even having to leave the hotel.'

Benefit statements should not however be used to pressurise clients into making a booking. An unsuitable holiday should not be pressed onto a client because this could mean that the client would cancel when they reconsidered the holiday later. Worse, they may take the holiday and return with a list of complaints and grievances which the travel agent would have to sort out. Either way, the pressurised sale has no place in a travel agency.

◇ Activity 13.3 ◇

The *Benefits Game* for four or more players!

You will need two dice of different colours, and two sets of six cards of similar colours. The following information should be printed or written on the cards.

Six numbered cards of one colour

| 1 The flight takes one hour. |

| 2 A coach will meet you at the airport. |

| 3 The hotel is on a main road. |

| 4 You will have half board in the hotel. |

| 5 The railway station is ten minutes walk from the hotel. |

| 6 The return flight leaves at 8 p.m. |

Six numbered cards of the other colour

| 1 A couple in their early 30s with two children aged 2 and 4. |

| 2 A couple in their early 40s with a son of 14 years. |

| 3 A retired couple in their 60s. |

| 4 A single parent with her 8-year-old daughter. |

| 5 A group of five single people aged 19 years. |

| 6 A honeymoon couple in their 20s. |

◊ *How to Play* ◊

Each player in turn will throw one dice. The player with the highest score will begin the game by throwing two dice. The two numbers thrown will indicate the cards to be used. For example, if the player throws four in colour one and three in colour two, the cards to be used will be, 'You will have half board in the hotel' and 'A retired couple'. The selected cards should be read aloud to the other players.

The player now has to turn the description on the first card into a benefit statement for the client on the second card, by using a linking phrase such as, 'which means that . . .'

Once the player has said a benefit statement, the other players will agree a score of **1** for an adequate statement, **2** for a good statement or **3** for a really outstanding benefit statement.

Play will continue with the person to the left throwing the two dice. The first player will be responsible for keeping the score.

The game ends when any player reaches 25 marks, or another agreed target, and is declared the winner.

Closing the Sale

The object of the earlier points is to elicit a commitment from the client. Ideally the client will pay a deposit and make a firm booking, but, failing this, the travel agent should try to get the client to take out an option.

If a client takes out an option on a holiday, the travel agent should make a note of their name, address and telephone number so that the contact can be renewed if the client fails to return. The travel agent should avoid finishing a potential sale with the client promising to get in touch, unless the travel agent has the means of making that contact possible.

The client who is ready to make a commitment will often give the travel agent a sign or clue by using a phrase such as, 'That sounds fine', or, 'Right, that's OK'. The travel agent should now close the sale with an assumption that the client is committed.

It would not be helpful to use a closed question such as, 'Would you like me to see if it is available?', because this could prompt a negative response. It would be far better to assume the client is going to book and say, 'I'll make a provisional booking for you'. At this stage fear could even be used as a stimulus by saying, 'I suggest you book now to avoid disappointment.' This is a form of pressurised selling and should really only be used when an indecisive client has to be encouraged to make a final decision.

If Viewdata is being used, the travel agent could indicate the details on screen, which will probably be personalised with the client's own name. Seeing the details on the screen and being invited to book now while the holiday is available will stimulate most people into a decision.

Other ways of closing the sale would be:

♦ by directly asking the client if they are ready to pay the deposit today;

♦ to physically pick up the phone or dial into a Viewdata system to check the availability;

♦ if several alternative holidays have been discussed, the client can be invited to make a choice so that the booking can be made.

If the client still hesitates at making a decision, the travel agent could summarise the details again and ask if there is anything else they might need. The client may simply need encouragement, time to discuss the arrangements with another person, or they may indeed have a genuine objection. If the client continues to ask questions then the situation can be clarified. If they do not, then the agent may have to ask more questions to investigate needs which have been left unstated.

For the client who raises actual objections, the travel agent's best approach is to agree to those objections as far as possible, but to use them to state benefits. For example, if the client says the apartments seem to be away from the shops, the travel agent might say, 'Yes, there is a short walk to the shops, but that makes it quieter at night because you are away from the discos and bars.' If the client says the holiday is too expensive, the agent should offer a cheaper one but should also point out the benefits which will be lost.

Whatever the objections, the travel agent should listen, try to clarify the situation and use open questions which will elicit more information. If the client says, 'I was wondering about the luggage allowance', try to clarify the problem by asking what they intended to take with them.

Once objections have been overcome the travel agent should recap on the details of the arrangements and make sure that they have all necessary information about the client.

Dealing with Difficult Clients

♦ The first thing to remember about difficult clients is that they probably do not see themselves as being difficult.

♦ The second thing to remember is that their awkwardness is probably part of their makeup, whether it be a result of their personality or just nervousness, and they act the same way with everyone.

So do not take it personally if a client is difficult with you and take consolation in remembering that they will probably be just as awkward with someone else within the same week or even on the same day. Try to handle the situation tactfully and, if necessary, refer to a senior assistant or the manager.

The *indecisive client* can be very difficult to deal with. However they may simply want their self-confidence boosted a little and to do this the travel agent should emphasise the benefits of the arrangements. With indecisive clients it is usually more useful to use closed rather than open questions. If this is done with skilful questions which inspire a, 'Yes', the client can be helped to make a decision.

Another potential client who can be difficult to deal with is the person who says they are, '*Just looking*'. Usually this really means that they do not want to be pounced on and so they should be approached with caution. With the browsing client, the travel agent should be observant and try to identify the clients' interests, by the brochures which take their eye, then build on this with further information or a few specific facts.

Disagreeable people will enter the travel agency at some time, whether they are angry about a problem or are just abrupt, argumentative or unreasonable by nature. The golden rule is to avoid antagonism with these people and to make an effort to listen. With disagreeable clients, sales talk should be kept to a minimum and questions should only be asked to clarify a situation. If the client is angry about a particular incident or problem, the conversation should be guided to the future and what can be done, rather than repeating details of a bad experience. Junior staff should always remember to refer a serious problem to more senior staff.

Talkative clients can be irritating, and the secret with them is to listen at first, until an interest has been identified. The travel agent should then attempt to take control by using conversational gaps to get straight to the point. With talkative clients, sales talk should be kept to a minimum, as should questions. If a sale is to be made however, the conversation should be maintained in a pleasant and courteous manner. Direction can be given to the conversation with clear choices being offered to the client, such as, 'Which hotel would you like in Fuengirola?' rather than a vague, 'So you have decided on Fuengirola . . .'. The tone of voice is as important as the words, because a business-like attitude, rather than a chatty, intimate atmosphere will achieve the close of sale more easily.

◊ *Revision Questions* ◊

1 Give two ways in which a potential client might be attracted or enticed into entering your travel agency.

2 Give three points to be taken into account when greeting a potential client.

3 Which two items or selling tools will you usually have at hand when trying to sell a holiday?

4 Once you have welcomed a potential client, which three stages do you need to consider if you are to sell a holiday?

5 In a display, which colours could be associated with the following?
a) Christmas
b) Cruising
c) Autumn
d) Calmness and freshness
e) Sunshine.

6 How many displayed brochures are usually needed to produce one firm booking?

7 Give two good reasons for keeping a tidy desk or counter in a travel agency.

8 A travel agent sells by stressing benefits which satisfy a particular client's specific needs. For a group of five young people aged 17 to 19, rewrite each of the following statements to emphasise the benefits.
a) The hotel has two restaurants and a coffee shop.
b) There is an excellent disco in the basement of the hotel.
c) The return flight leaves at 8 p.m.
d) You will have half-board in the hotel.
e) There is no real beach, but you can swim from the rocks near to the hotel.

9 Describe two ways in which you could attempt to close a sale with a client who is hesitant.

10 Which two courses of action would you take with an angry client who has come to complain about a bad experience on a holiday which you had booked?

Conclusion

Where do we go from here?

In the introduction we said that this course of study was primarily aimed at those who wished to work in a travel agency. The role of a travel agent is really central to the travel industry as we know it in Britain. Almost every section of the industry comes into contact with a travel agent at some time. Travel agents are used by all the following to sell their products:

♦ tour operators to sell their holidays,
♦ coach operators to sell excursions,
♦ charter airlines to sell flight only bookings,
♦ schedule airlines to sell airline tickets,
♦ National Express,
♦ British Rail,
♦ car ferries,
♦ car hire companies,
♦ insurance companies . . . and the list could go on!

Not only is the travel agency central to the industry but it is also an excellent training ground for jobs in almost any area of travel. The skills outlined in this book inlcude:

♦ a knowledge of travel geography,
♦ an awareness of the tourist industry,
♦ the ability to create a brochure costing,
♦ an awareness of the implications of travel law,
♦ marketing skills,
♦ office practices,
♦ selling skills and
♦ dealing with difficult clients.

These skills are a basis for careers in many areas both inside and outside the travel industry. With two years experience in a travel agency, the natural maturity which those years would bring and a thorough knowledge and experience of the above skills a person would be well-qualified to move into other areas of travel such as:

♦ courier work abroad,
♦ brochure production with a tour operator,
♦ litigation department with a tour operator,
♦ sales with BR, car ferries or car hire,
♦ ground handling at an airport,
♦ air steward or a
♦ steward on a cruise ship . . . and many more!

For the person who is keen and interested in travel and can master the basic knowledge and skills the world is their oyster!

Glossary of Terms

Ad hoc is a term used when reservations are made, as and when required by individual clients. For example, the travel agent would have to telephone or telex a hotel to make the reservation rather than make the booking from a previously agreed allocation.

Allocation is a block of hotel rooms or airline seats which are made available to a tour operator or travel agent. The rooms or seats are reserved in their name until an agreed release date.

American Plan (AP) is accommodation with breakfast and two main meals included in the price.

Back-to-back is a term used to describe the practice of charter airlines whereby an aircraft flies out with a full load of passengers and returns with another full load who have completed their holiday.

Bond is a type of insurance taken out by a travel company, possibly with a bank, so that, if the travel company ceases trading, costs can be recovered to compensate clients who are stranded abroad or who may have lost their holiday or flight.

Break even point is the holiday price which a tour operator needs to charge to cover minimum costs.

Business house is a travel agency which specialises in serving local firms with travel arrangements, visas and currency exchange.

Charter aircraft are commissioned for a specific period of time and usually fly with a full load of passengers to a given destination.

Collision damage waiver is an extra insurance cover which clients who are hiring a car should be advised to take. This covers the costs for the client in the event of an accident without prejudicing their own UK car cover.

Commission is payment made to a travel agent by principals such as tour operators, airlines, ferry companies and car hire firms. The payment made is a percentage of the value of the booking. The percentage of commission paid varies from one principal to another.

Confirmed is the term used for a booking for which a client has paid the deposit.

Consolidation occurs when clients are asked to change their flight or hotel arrangements by a tour operator who has poor bookings. For example, bookings may be poor from both Manchester and Birmingham airports and clients from one airport are required to use the other airport so that one full load of passengers can depart on one aircraft.

Continental Plan (CP) is accommodation with breakfast included in the price.

Contract is an agreement between two parties. The agreement may be written, oral or implied.

Controllable costs are those such as lighting, heating, telephone calls and stationery items, which can be used or abused by the staff of a travel company.

Corporate image is the image or impression given of a company. The impression given is promoted by advertising, logo and the attitude of its staff.

Courier is a representative of the tour operator who is employed to assist clients on package holidays. For example, a courier will meet clients at the airport, assist with general enquiries, and make arrangements for clients who are ill, to see a local doctor.

Density is a measurement of the space available on a ship in relation to each passenger. To calculate the density, the Gross Registered Tonnage of the vessel should be divided by the number of passengers to be carried.

Deposit is a small payment per person made by a client to secure a holiday or travel booking. A deposit is normally not refundable. The balance of payment is usually due eight weeks before the departure date.

Domestic is the term applied to flights and holidays in the United Kingdom. It applies to mainland Britain, Northern Ireland, and the off-shore islands.

Empty legs are those flights made by charter aircraft without passengers at the beginning and end of the season. The first flight out in a season will have to return without passengers, and also the last flight out will be made solely to pick up holidaymakers who have completed their stay.

European Plan (EP) is accommodation, but no meals included in the price.

Excursionist is used to describe people who travel for pleasure or make a visit for only a day, without staying overnight away from their normal place of residence.

Ex gratia payment is sometimes made by a tour operator or airline when a problem has arisen for a client. Such a payment is made on the understanding that the principal does not accept any liability or responsibility for what has gone wrong, but is simply making the payment as a goodwill gesture.

Expiry date is the date after which an option or booking will not be reserved for a client.

Fixed costs are costs such as staff salaries, rent or mortgage payments which have to be paid for by a travel company.

Flight series means charter aircraft which are made available to a tour operator at a specific time each day, or week, for a specific number of flights.

Fly/cruise is a term used to describe package holidays which include a client's flight to the Mediterranean, Caribbean or another area, in order to take a cruise.

Fly/drive is the term used to describe package holidays where the client flies out to a holiday destination and a hire car is waiting for them at the airport. This type of holiday very often involves independent travel making use of hotel vouchers for accommodation.

Force majeure or, 'Acts of God', are circumstances beyond the control of a tour operator which may force a change to be made to holiday arrangements. For example, a hurricane, threat of war, nuclear disaster or terrorist activity.

Gateway airport is the airport through which the majority of tourists fly into a resort or area.

Gîtes are self-catering units in France which have been modernised with help from the French government and are supervised and let by the Fédération Nationale des Gîtes.

Ground arrangements are the services provided by a tour operator in the resort for their package holidaymakers. The ground arrangements are usually organised by the courier and include taking the clients to their accommodation and offering excursions or car hire.

High, or peak, season refers to the most popular dates for flights or holidays. The most expensive prices apply to these dates. The other seasons are called low and shoulder seasons.

IIT means **independent inclusive tours** and refers to package holidays prepared and sold by travel agents using commission rates from principals in transport and hotels.

Inbound tour operators provide holidays for foreigners coming into their country. Inbound tour operators in Britain can join BITOA, the British Incoming Tour Operators Association. Other countries have their own inbound tour operators, such as Intourist which is the inbound tour operator for the Soviet Union.

Incentive commission is a higher rate of commission paid by tour operators or other principals to stimulate more sales by a travel agent who already has a higher than average turnover of business for them.

Infrastructure refers to the roads, buildings, airport and other permanent facilities provided in a holiday destination.

ITC means **inclusive tours by charter** and is used to describe package holidays which make use of chartered aircraft.

ITX means **inclusive tours by excursion** and refers to package holidays which make use of seats on scheduled aircraft which have been made available to the tour operator at SGITS.

Lead name is the name of the first person on a booking form. This person should sign the booking form and for legal reasons should be over the age of eighteen.

Leakage describes the situation where tourists' money does not remain in a host country because it is used to pay off national debts, to provide profits for foreign airlines or hotels, or to pay the wages of non-nationals.

Load factor is the number of airline seats or hotel beds sold as a percentage of the number available. Airlines and tour operators calculate their prices based on a minimum load factor, that is the minimum number of clients required to break even and cover costs.

Long haul describes destinations beyond Europe. For example, India, the Far East, the USA and Canada are all long haul destinations.

Long stay holiday means a holiday of more than two or three weeks. Such holidays are taken by some tourists in the winter and may last for up to three months.

Low season refers to the least popular dates for flights or holidays. The cheapest prices will apply to these dates. The other seasons are called high, or peak, season and shoulder season.

Market segmentation is concerned with the part of the general public that is likely to be interested in a product or holiday.

Mark-up is a percentage of 20 to 35 per cent which is added to the basic cost of a holiday by a tour operator to cover fixed costs, travel agent's commission and profit.

Medium haul describes destinations within Europe. For example, Rome, Athens and the Costa del Sol are all medium haul destinations. Medium haul destinations are sometimes referred to as short haul.

Modified American Plan (MAP) is accommodation with breakfast and one main meal included in the price.

Multiplier effect describes the means by which tourists' money spreads to all sections of society and tourism benefits the economy of the host country.

Option is a term used to describe a holiday booking which has been reserved for a client. The option will be held for a specific period of time, such as 24 hours, to give the client time to send the deposit and confirm the booking.

Option form is used by travel agents to record details of a client's request. Information such as the client's name, the desired resort and hotel, the departure date and airport would all be recorded on the form.

Option reference is the reference number for a booking given by the tour operator to the travel agent. This number should be carefully recorded so that it can be quoted when the client pays the deposit and confirms the holiday.

Outbound tour operators produce package holidays for UK residents wishing to holiday abroad.

Overrider commission is extra commission paid by a tour operator to a travel agent who does more than average business for them. The overrider commission could be two or three per cent over the usual ten per cent offered by the tour operator.

Package holidays are put together by tour operators who charge an all-in price for the whole holiday including transport, accommodation, transfers and the services of a courier.

Passenger manifest is a list of names of passengers in an hotel, or on an aircraft or ship.

Peak or high season, refers to the most popular dates for flights or holidays. The most expensive prices apply to these dates. The other seasons are called low and shoulder seasons.

Pipeline money is money which has been paid to a travel agent by a client but which has not as yet been sent on to the principal.

Principal is the general term used to describe companies with whom a travel agent may do business. A principal may be a tour operator, an airline, a ferry company or a car hire firm.

Receipt is a written acknowledgement of an amount of money received from a client. Receipts should have serial numbers so that each one can be accounted for, and they should be issued for all transactions, whether by cash, cheque or credit card.

Reconciliation is the calculation at the end of a period of time, such as on a daily or monthly basis, of the amount of money taken and paid out by a company.

Reference is the identification of the person or company with whom a booking has been made. Very often the reference is the first name of that person.

Release date is the date after which an airline or hotel is free to sell seats or beds if the tour operator has not taken the full quota of their allocation.

Scheduled flights operate to a timetable and are committed to fly whether or not the aircraft is full.

Self-catering holidays include accommodation with kitchen facilities, but no meals.

Short haul destinations are those closest to home such as northern France, Belgium, Holland and parts of Germany and Scandinavia. They can also include other European destinations such as Athens, Rome etc., which are usually classed as medium haul destinations.

Shoulder season refers to the dates for flights or holidays which are neither the most nor the least popular. For example, the shoulder season for transatlantic flights covers the autumn rather than summer or Christmas. The other seasons are called high, or peak, season and low season.

SGITS means **special group inclusive tour rates** and these are specially priced scheduled airline seats made available to tour operators who wish to offer **ITX**.

Stabiliser is the agreement of ABTA members that, with regard to foreign package holidays, ABTA travel agents will only deal with ABTA tour operators and vice versa.

Tender means using a small boat, very often utilising the life boats, to ferry from a cruise ship to the quayside.

Time charter means that an aircraft is made available to a tour operator over a period of time, such as six or twelve months.

Tort is a Norman-French word which simply means a wrong. In law in Britain the word is used to identify wrongs which are serious enough to merit damages being awarded but which are not actually criminal offences.

Tourist is a person who travels for pleasure, staying one or more nights in a place other than their normal place of residence.

Tour operators package and sell holidays which are offered in a brochure with a fixed price for accommodation, transport and ground arrangements.

Transfer is the transport provided by tour operators to take their clients from the airport or port to their accommodation.

Travel agents book holidays or travel arrangements for clients. The travel agent also offers advice with regard to destinations, passports, health regulations and visas. The main source of income for this service is the commission the travel agent receives from principals with whom the bookings are made.

Variable costs are costs which have to be taken into account by a tour operator when costing holidays, but which vary according to the number of people travelling. For example, these costs include the ticket and inflight refreshments.

Visa is a stamp in a passport giving the holder permission to enter or leave a country.

Index